W9-BSA-986

Sunset

136
BEST WAYS TO
SAVE
ON YOUR
HOME
ENERGY

BY THE EDITORS OF SUNSET BOOKS

MENLO PARK, CALIFORNIA

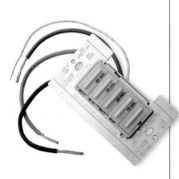

SUNSET BOOKS

Vice President, General Manager: Richard A. Smeby
Vice President, Editorial Director: Bob Doyle
Production Director: Lory Day
Director of Operations: Rosann Sutherland
Art Director: Vasken Guiragossian

Staff for this book
Editor: Lee Hassig
Art Director: Don Taka
Consulting Editors: Joseph Truini, Scott Atkinson, Bridget Biscotti Bradley,
    Marianne Lipanovich
Writers: Jeff Beneke, Steve Cory, Jim Lynch, Rick Peters, Glen Ruh,
    Lisa Stockwell Kessler
Copy Editor: Julie Harris
Proofreaders: Alicia Eckley, Carol Whiteley
Photo Researcher: Jane Martin
Computer Production: Linda M. Bouchard
Illustration: Marina Thompson, Anthony Davis, Rik Olson, Dartmouth Publishing, Inc.
Production Coordinators: Eligio Hernandez, Danielle Javier
Editorial Coordinator: Audrey Mak
Indexer: Nanette Cardon

Cover: Design by Vasken Guiragossian. Photography by Scott Atkinson (top, bottom)
    and Mark Rutherford (middle).

Photographers: **Scott Atkinson:** 1 middle, 2 top, 18, 22, 30 middle, 34, 36 top, 38, 39, 40 bottom, 41, 42, 43, 44 top and bottom, 45 bottom, 62, 63, 65, 67 top right, bottom left, bottom middle, bottom right, 69, 72 bottom left, bottom middle, bottom right, 75, 79, 80, 82, 90, back cover bottom left; **James Darell/Tony Stone Images:** 10; **Empire Comfort Systems:** 25; **Charles Gupton/The Stock Market:** 15; **Ken Gutmaker:** 16; **Everett C. Johnson/Folio, Inc.:** 29; **Llewellyn/Uniphoto:** 20; **E. Andrew McKinney:** 25; **Pictor Uniphoto:** 4 middle, 6, 7, 21; **Norman A. Plate:** 26; **Jon Riley/Folio, Inc.:** 9, 27; **Steve J. Romanik:** 48; **Mark Rutherford:** 2 bottom, 3, 28, 30 bottom, 31, 35, 36 bottom, 37, 40 top, 44 middle, 45 top, 60 bottom, 67 top left, 72 top, 73, 77, 84, 85, back cover right; **Dan Stultz:** 1 top and bottom, 30 top, 50, 52, 53, 55, 56, 57, 58, 60 top, back cover top left; **Superstock:** 4 top and bottom, 5, 8, 10, 11, 12, 13, 14, 17, 20, 28, 29, 30, 32; **The Stock Market:** 6; **Michael Ventura/Folio, Inc.:** 5; **Tom Wyatt:** 19, 24

10 9 8 7 6 5 4 3 2 1

First Printing September 2001
Copyright © 2001 Sunset Publishing Corporation, Menlo Park, CA 94025.

First Edition. All rights reserved, including the right of reproduction in whole or in part in any form. Library of Congress Control Number: 2001094547.
ISBN 0-376-01204-8.

Printed in the United States.

For additional copies of *136 Best Ways to Save on Your Home Energy* or any other Sunset book, call 1-800-526-5111 or visit us at www.sunsetbooks.com

CONTENTS

136 | ENERGY-SAVING TIPS

This is an action book. Beginning on the next page, you'll find 136 energy-saving tips that are proven to cut utility bills, sometimes substantially. Many of the simplest and least expensive measures can also be the most effective. For example, you're likely to save more money sooner by turning off unneeded lights than you will by replacing single-glazed windows with the double-glazed variety.

Of course, some cost-cutting measures require more than flipping a switch, and a few are best left to professionals. For the rest, you'll find detailed instructions begining on page 33. All the procedures are simple enough for beginners, and none require expensive tools.

Start now. Do one small thing today, then another tomorrow. The savings, though small, do add up. Before you know it, you'll have sliced a noticeable chunk from your energy bills—money that you can put to better use in another part of your household budget.

Use the legend below to interpret the symbols that appear at the end of each tip. Colored dots rate the tips according to how quickly you can apply them; dollar signs score them on bang-for-the-buck.

● Do It Now $ Good

● Get Out Your Tools $$ Better

● Consult a Pro $$$ Best

1 SWITCH OFF LIGHTS WHEN YOU LEAVE A ROOM

Households use 50 to 200 kilowatt-hours a month on lighting alone. By turning off three 75-watt lights that burn needlessly for two hours a day, you can shave as much as 2 percent from your lighting costs each month. $$$ ●

2 DUST YOUR LIGHT BULBS REGULARLY

Clean bulbs give off 50 percent more light than dirty ones, giving you all the light you're paying for. If that turns out to be more light than you need, try a smaller light bulb. $$$ ●

3 BUY THREE-WAY BULBS INSTEAD OF THE SINGLE-WATTAGE VARIETY

Three-way bulbs are the easiest, least-expensive way to dim lamps when you don't need full brightness. A three-way bulb will work in any lamp fitted with a switch that seems to have two ON and two OFF positions when a single-wattage bulb is screwed into the light bulb socket. $$ ●

4 USE ENERGY-SAVING NIGHT-LIGHTS

Instead of a 4-watt incandescent night-light, go for the cool, turquoise glow of an electroluminescent model. It consumes only $3/100$ watt, a 13,000 percent savings in electricity. For a brighter night-light, consider the mini-fluorescent variety. Rated at 7 watts, it puts out as much light as a 20-watt incandescent bulb. Some models include a battery backup system that provides emergency light in a blackout. $$$ ●

5 USE THE LOWEST-WATTAGE LIGHT BULBS POSSIBLE

Never use brighter bulbs than you need for a particular light fixture or task. Experiment with different bulbs to learn how bright a bulb you really need; brightness, expressed in lumens, appears on light bulb packages. When you shop for light bulbs, compare the output in lumens of different brands. High-efficiency bulbs—more lumens per watt—may let you use smaller, less power-hungry bulbs in some lamps. $$$ ●

6 MOVE LAMPS TOWARD CORNERS OF ROOMS

Place your lamps in the corners of rooms, where their light can reflect off two walls. You'll need fewer lights if you position them well and equip them with light-colored lamp shades. $$$ ●

7 ADD WINDOWS FOR MORE LIGHT

It may pay to install more windows in dark rooms, especially when renovating a house extensively. Check window costs with your contractor to judge how long windows will take to pay for themselves in lower electric bills. Some states limit the number of windows you can have in your home; consult your building department for more information. $ ●

8 GET RID OF HALOGEN TORCHÈRES

Halogen floor lamps, or torchères, are one of the most inefficient light sources available. A torchère fitted with a 36-watt CFL (page 7) will produce 25 percent more light than a 300-watt halogen torchère, using only one-fourth the energy. Switching can save up to $250 over the life of the lamp. $$ ●

9 ADD DIMMERS TO YOUR LAMPS AND LIGHT CIRCUITS

The less power you supply to your lights, the more money you'll save on your electric bill. Dimmers permit you to adjust the brightness of your lights according to your needs by reducing the flow of electricity. It's easy to replace a wall switch with a dimmer (page 38) or to add one to a lamp cord (page 39). $ ●

10 PAINT YOUR WALLS LIGHT COLORS

Whites, off-whites, and pastels reflect light better than darker tones. After repainting, you may be able to swap 75-watt bulbs for 100-watters in many lamps—and knock 25 percent off the cost of using each one. $ ●

11 TAKE BETTER ADVANTAGE OF DAYLIGHT

Working by natural light adds nothing to your lighting costs. If you have window coverings, open them up; or hang white, translucent curtains that let in the light without sacrificing privacy. Move your desk or the chairs you use for reading nearer to the windows. $$$ ●

12 EMPHASIZE TASK LIGHTING

Why light up a whole room when you're working in only a small part of it? Save money and waste less energy with good desk, reading, and under-counter lamps or fixtures that focus light just where it's needed. $$ ●

13 BUY COMPACT FLUORESCENT LAMPS INSTEAD OF INCANDESCENT BULBS

Despite "lamp" in the name, these remarkable lighting devices, called CFLs, are actually fluorescent light bulbs.

They cost significantly more than incandescent bulbs, but they last ten times longer. Better yet, they require 75 percent less energy than incandescents to produce the same amount of light. For every 100-watt incandescent bulb you replace with a 36-watt CFL, you can save $25 or more in energy costs over the lifetime of such a bulb.

These energy-efficient bulbs come in oval and spiral shapes to fit

almost any lighting fixture, and they create a more natural light than fluorescent tubes of the past. Some CFLs are designed for outdoor use; they are ideal as replacements for incandescent bulbs in pathway lighting, for example.

In addition, CFLs produce light at temperatures below 100°F. As a result, they have less impact on your cooling costs during hot weather than incandescents, which convert 90 percent of the energy they consume to heat and become hot enough to ignite paper and cloth.

The table below shows the energy requirements of incandescent bulbs and Energy Star CFLs that produce comparable brightness, usually expressed in lumens. CFLs produce 40 to 60 lumens per watt compared with 8 to 18 lumens per watt for incandescent bulbs. $$ ●

Incandescent Bulbs (watts)	Compact Fluorescent Lamps (watts)
40	10
60	15
75	20
100	25

14 REGULATE ELECTRIC DEVICES WITH AUTOMATIC TIMERS

To control the electricity consumed by such items as bathroom heat lamps, ceiling and attic fans, spa jets, as well as pool pumps and heaters, install timer switches for these items to turn them on and off at set times of the day (page 40). $$ ●

15 LIGHT YOUR WORKSHOP EFFICIENTLY

If you light your workshop, garage, or shed with incandescent bulbs, switch to fluorescents. Choose a fixture that has an electronic ballast. It extends the life of fluorescent tubes by 40 to 100 percent, eliminates distracting flicker, and permits dimming of fluorescent lights to less than 1 percent of their maximum output. $$ ●

16 INSTALL MOTION DETECTORS, TIMERS, OR PHOTOELECTRIC SENSORS TO CONTROL OUTDOOR LIGHTING

If you often forget to turn off outdoor lights during the day, you can save money on your electric bill by turning them on and off automatically. For example, if you install a timer in the circuit (page 40), you can set it to turn lights on as you go to bed and off when you wake in the morning. Or replace an ordinary outdoor floodlight fixture with one that has a motion detector (page 42); it turns the lights on when it senses movement, then off again after an adjustable interval. To keep lights from coming on before dusk, add a photoelectric sensor to the circuit (page 45). $$ ●

17 GO SOLAR IN THE GARDEN OR USE FLUORESCENTS

You pay nothing for electricity that comes from the sun. Several manufacturers offer solar-powered exterior lights that illuminate pathways, stairwells, and plants. Some are even bright enough to provide security lighting. In these systems, electricity generated by sunlight falling on photovoltaic (solar) cells is stored in

rechargeable batteries for use at night. Self-contained units that have the photovoltaic module atop the light fixture require a sunny location. Other systems provide a separate photovoltaic panel that can be located in direct sunlight, apart from the light fixtures. $$ ●

18 PUT YOUR COMPUTER AND PERIPHERALS TO SLEEP WHEN NOT IN USE

You can instruct newer computers—as well as monitors, printers, scanners, copiers, and fax machines—to switch automatically into an energy-saving "sleep" mode if the device is idle for a prescribed length of time. In this mode, computer equipment consumes much less power and runs cooler than when fully awake. If the sleep mode doesn't work well with your computer—or if you have older equipment without this feature—turn the machines off when they're not in use. $$$ ●

A Sign of Efficiency

The U.S. Environmental Protection Agency's Energy Star labeling program establishes energy-efficiency standards for a variety of office equipment, home appliances, and other power-hungry devices. By purchasing Energy Star products when remodeling or upgrading homes, offices, and businesses over the next decade, Americans can trim their national energy bill by about $200 billion annually, according to EPA estimates.

The program began in 1992 with specifications for personal computers and monitors. Since then, it has expanded beyond the U.S., and standards now govern clothes- and dishwashers, windows, roofing materials, entire buildings, and even traffic signals—among many other things.

The Energy Star label on a product certifies that it is at least 13 percent more energy efficient than comparable products without the label. In some cases, energy use is more than halved. Such performance may cost somewhat more to buy, but the difference in price is more than repaid through energy savings over the life of the product. Moreover, many utility companies offer rebates on Energy Star appliances, making them more affordable.

19 INVEST IN POWER-SAVING CONTROLLERS FOR MOTOR-DRIVEN APPLIANCES

For less than $40 you can buy a plug-in microcontroller that lets an appliance with an induction motor—such as a refrigerator, freezer, window air conditioner, or furnace fan, run cooler and more quietly on less electricity. This microcontroller, called the Energy-Smart Power Planner and manufactured by CEM Industries, is intended for older appliances; newer ones often have a microcontroller built in. The device comes in 8-, 10-, and 20-amp models to handle almost any household appliance that has an induction motor. $$ ●

20 REPLACE YOUR OLD COPIER WITH AN ENERGY STAR MODEL

Copiers cost more to run than any other office equipment. Energy Star models not only have a reduced-power mode that can lower your electric bill, but they also offer a double-sided-copy feature that saves paper and electricity. $ ●

21 LOOK FOR THE ENERGY STAR LABEL WHEN REPLACING OLD APPLIANCES

When you need a new appliance, look for the Energy Star label. These high-efficiency appliances have a 30- to 90-percent improvement in energy efficiency over those made in 1980. They cost more than less-efficient models, but the long-term savings more than compensate. For instance, an Energy Star refrigerator will pay for itself in energy savings in just over three years and save you much more money over its lifetime. $$$ ●

22 KEEP YOUR REFRIGERATOR FULL

The mass of the contents, once they are cooled, helps hold the temperature down. $$$ ●

23 KEEP YOUR REFRIGERATOR COOL

When a refrigerator is surrounded by warm air, its compressor must work overtime. A decrease of 5°F in ambient air temperature can cut energy consumption by 20 percent. To keep your refrigerator cool, allow about 2 inches of airspace between the appliance and nearby walls and cabinets; doing so offers an escape route for heat from the compressor and condensing coils. Shield your refrigerator from direct sunlight, and position it as far as practical from the oven, stove, dishwasher, and heating vent.

Do not, however, place the refrigerator in an unheated area. In temperatures below 55°F, the compressor many not run long or often enough to keep the freezer cold. $$$ ●

24 TURN OFF THE ICEMAKER IN YOUR FREEZER

The convenience of ice at your fingertips can increase energy consumption by 14 to 20 percent. Make ice the old fashioned way—in ice trays. $$$ ●

25 SET THE REFRIGERATOR AND FREEZER FOR THE IDEAL TEMPERATURES

Super-cold temperatures in a refrigerator or freezer offer little benefit and waste energy. To minimize the amount of money you spend to keep food cold, keep the refrigerator temperature between 37 and 40°F and the freezer between 0 and 5°F. To check the refrigerator temperature, place a thermometer in a glass of water, and set it in the refrigerator for 24 hours. To check the freezer, place the thermometer between frozen foods for the same amount of time. $$$ ●

26 CLOSE THE REFRIGERATOR DOOR

Each minute you stand in front of an open refrigerator contemplating its contents is money flowing out the door. $$$ ●

27 CHECK REFRIGERATOR AND FREEZER DOORS FOR A GOOD SEAL

Magnetic door seals can weaken their grip on the edge of the refrigerator or freezer cabinet. Test the seals regularly by closing a piece of paper in each door at several places around the perimeter. If the paper pulls out easily, the seal is weak. You may need to adjust the door or install a new seal (page 47). $$ ●

28 KEEP REFRIGERATED FOODS COVERED

Covering foods not only keeps flavors from mixing but also reduces power consumption by limiting the evaporation of moisture into the air. Moist air, harder to cool than dry air, forces the compressor to work for longer periods of time. $$$ ●

29 RETIRE YOUR 10-YEAR-OLD REFRIGERATOR

A refrigerator consumes more electricity than any other appliance in your home. But a modern Energy Star model that uses less than half the energy of a 10-year-old refrigerator can cut your household energy expenditures by as much as 4½ percent.

The most efficient refrigerators are 16- to 20-cubic-foot models, but if you need more cold storage than that, it's cheaper to operate one large refrigerator than two small ones. Refrigerators with the freezer on top consume 7 to 13 percent less electricity than side-by-side models. In the near future, a 20½-cubic-foot refrigerator of this design will use the same power as a 50-watt light bulb. Manual-defrost refrigerators sip electricity at half the rate of those that defrost automatically, but you must defrost them regularly to realize the savings.

Look for a refrigerator with automatic moisture control. This feature prevents condensation on the outside, eliminating the need for a built-in heater to control this nuisance. The heater adds as much as 10 percent to the cost of running the appliance. $$ ●

How to Buy an Efficient Appliance

It's tempting to shop for appliances by price alone, but any appliance purchase packs a double economic punch—the cost of buying it and the cost of operating it. With major appliances lasting from 10 to 20 years and energy prices on the rise, buying the least-expensive model can be a false economy, since less-expensive versions are often less efficient as well. The difference in efficiency can impose unnecessary energy costs. Over the years, they can amount to several times the difference in purchase price between a less-efficient appliance and a more-efficient one.

To help you make the best purchase decision possible, the Energy Guide label (below), pasted prominently on major appliances, as well as heating and cooling equipment, reveals how a particular appliance compares in efficiency with others like it. Near the top of the label appear the type of appliance used in the comparison (1)—top-loading clothes washers here—as well as the model numbers to which the label applies (2). When shopping, confirm that the label on any appliance you are considering is the one that belongs there.

A box in the center of the label (3) estimates the energy—in kilowatt-hours for washers—you can expect this machine to consume each year. The amount appears along a scale that places the most-efficient washers on the left and the least efficient on the right. This one falls in the middle of the pack.

Below the energy-use comparison appears an estimate of the annual operating cost, including heating the wash water (4). Because water may be heated either electrically or with gas, the label gives two cost figures.

The basis for all this information appears at the bottom of the label (5). In all likelihood, your cost of energy and pattern of appliance use will differ from these assumptions. Thus, the energy consumed by this machine in your home, as well as its operating costs, could be less or more than the figures on the label. $$$ ●

Based on standard U.S. Government tests

ENERGYGUIDE

Refrigerator-Freezer
With Automatic Defrost
With Top-Mounted Freezer
Without Through-The-Door Ice Service
Capacity: 21.5 Cubic Feet

KitchenAid
Models: KTRC22KK**0*,
KTRC22EK**0*

Compare the Energy Use of this Refrigerator with Others Before You Buy.

This Model Uses 472kWh/year		ENERGY STAR A symbol of energy efficiency

Energy use (kWh/year) range of all similar models

Uses Least Energy 559	ENERGY STAR refrigerators use at least 10% less energy annually than the Federal Maximum.	Uses Most Energy 767

The Estimated Annual Energy Consumption of this model was not available at the time the range was published.

kWh/year (kilowatt-hours per year) is a measure of energy (electricity) use. Your utility company uses it to compute your bill. Only models with 20.5 to 22.4 cubic feet and the above features are used in this scale.

Refrigerators using more energy cost more to operate. This model's estimated yearly operating cost is:

$40

Based on a 1998 U.S. Government national average cost of 8.42¢ per kWh for electricity. Your actual operating cost will vary depending on your local utility rates and your use of the product.

Important: Removal of this label before consumer purchase violates the Federal Trade Commission's Appliance Labeling Rule (16 CFR Part 305). 2218072

Put the electric can opener, juice squeezer, and egg beater in the cupboard, and save money by doing as many kitchen tasks manually as you can. $$$ ●

31 **VACUUM YOUR REFRIGERATOR'S CONDENSER COILS ANNUALLY**

When condenser coils are clean, the compressor cools more efficiently and runs less frequently. Pull your refrigerator away from the wall and vacuum the coils behind it (page 46). If the coils are underneath the refrigerator, remove the grille at the bottom of the appliance and brush the coils. $$$ ●

32 AIR-DRY YOUR HAIR

A 1,500-watt hair dryer uses 375 watt-hours of power every 15 minutes. Save by letting your hair dry naturally. $$$ ●

33 KEEP THE GAS FLAMES IN YOUR KITCHEN BURNING BLUE

In gas stoves, ovens, water heaters, and the like, blue flames mean efficient burning. If flames are yellow, try increasing the air supply (page 48). $$$ ●

34 DEFROST FOOD BEFORE COOKING IT

You can lop 30 to 50 percent off the cost of cooking a dish by starting with food that has been defrosted in the refrigerator overnight or at room temperature for several hours. $$$ ●

35 STEAM VEGETABLES INSTEAD OF BOILING THEM TO SAVE ENERGY AND WATER

Steaming cooks vegetables faster than boiling them, and they retain more vitamins and minerals. Use only ¼ cup of water for fastest cooking time. A pressure cooker, which steams food at temperatures exceeding 250ºF, cuts cooking time in half. $$$ ●

36 MATCH THE PAN TO THE BURNER

When you place a small pan on a large burner, all the heat outside the edges of the pan is wasted. Put small pans on small burners; save the others for large pots and skillets. If you have a gas stove, you can turn down the flame to keep it from curling around the sides of your smallest pans. $$$ ●

37 KEEP YOUR STOVE-TOP REFLECTORS SHINY

Heat from stove-top burners radiates downward as well as upward. The purpose of reflectors below the burners is to redirect heat toward the pan. Keep reflectors clean and shiny; they will reflect heat better and cook food faster at less cost.

An easy way to keep reflectors sparkling is to cover them with aluminum foil, shiny side up. When the foil becomes stained, replace it. $$$ ●

38 BAKE AN ENTIRE MEAL AT ONE TIME

To economize on oven use, plan meals so that the main dish, vegetables, and dessert can be baked at the same time or in close succession. Use your oven's convection feature, if it has one, to cook all the dishes evenly. $$$ ●

39 COVER PANS FOR FASTER COOKING

When you put a lid on a pan, you trap heat inside, reducing the time it takes to bring water to a boil and to cook your food. And you save money in the bargain. If you want to keep water hot but not boiling for any length of time, turn the heat down to low. Turn the heat up, and the water will come to a boil again in short order. $$$ ●

40 TRY TURNING OFF ELECTRIC BURNERS AND OVENS 5 MINUTES BEFORE THE FOOD IS DONE

Ovens, electric stove-top heating elements, and many newer gas burners stay hot for many minutes after you turn them off. Save electricity or gas and the money it costs by taking advantage of this heat to finish cooking your food. $$$ ●

41 BAKE POTATOES AND OTHER SMALL ITEMS IN A TOASTER OVEN

Countertop ovens take no longer to cook food than a full-size electric oven, but they consume only one-third the power. $$$ ●

42 COOK WITH A MICROWAVE OVEN WHENEVER POSSIBLE

A microwave saves money on two fronts. First, it cooks food up to six times faster than an electric oven—and draws about ⅓ the electricity. Second, it helps lower air-conditioning costs by keeping the kitchen cool on hot summer days. $$$ ●

43 DON'T PEEK INTO THE OVEN DURING COOKING

Valuable heat escapes from the oven every time you open the door. If it has a window and if there's an oven light switch on the control panel, it's easy to check on cooking progress without opening the door. When testing for doneness with a fast-acting thermometer, take the dish out of the oven and close the door. $$$ ●

44 TRY BAKING WITHOUT PRE-HEATING THE OVEN

Don't waste money bringing the oven to cooking temperature before placing food inside. Because many new ovens are well insulated, they heat up so rapidly that they can bake—or broil—foods from a cold start. You won't even have to lengthen the cooking time. $$$ ●

45 DEGREASE THE OVEN DOOR SEAL

A tight seal between the oven door and the cabinet will ensure maximum heat retention. Gently clean the seal and the cabinet where they meet with hot, sudsy water or a general-purpose kitchen cleaner, dabbing the liquid onto the mesh seal with a cloth. Take care not to move or damage the seal. $$$ ●

13

46 WHEN PURCHASING A GAS STOVE OR OVEN, LOOK FOR PILOTLESS IGNITION

Nearly half the money spent on gas for a typical pilot-lit stove or oven goes to keeping the eternal flame of the pilot light burning. An electric ignition system requires no pilot light. In a power failure, you can light the stove and oven with a match. $$ ●

47 WHEN PURCHASING A NEW DISHWASHER, LOOK FOR AN INTERNAL WATER HEATER AND MINIMUM WATER USAGE

A dishwasher that heats its own water can slash 20 percent from the cost of heating water for your entire household. Because the dishwasher raises the water temperature to the recommended 140°F and keeps it there, you can lower your water-heater temperature to 120°F. If you also select a dishwasher that requires no more than 15 gallons of water per full-wash cycle, you'll reduce both your water consumption and water-heating costs. $$ ●

48 SCRAPE DISHES, DON'T RINSE THEM

Rinsing dishes before you put them in the dishwasher wastes water and the energy used to heat it. Newer dishwashers clean better, eliminating the need for pre-rinsing unless food is baked or dried onto plates or pans. $$ ●

49 USE YOUR DISHWASHER'S ENERGY-SAVER FEATURE OR AIR-DRY YOUR DISHES

Modern dishwashers allow you to turn off the heated drying cycle. Doing so halves the energy used for a load of dishes. If this energy-saving feature is absent, stop the machine after the final rinse, and open the door partway to air-dry the dishes. $$$ ●

50 RUN THE SHORTEST CYCLE POSSIBLE

Experiment with your dishwasher's settings until you find the cycle that does a satisfactory job in the shortest time. $$$ ●

51 RUN THE DISHWASHER ONLY WHEN IT'S FULL

A dishwasher consumes the same amount of energy to wash one dish as to wash a full load, so fill the dishwasher before running it. However, do not overfill. Dishes stacked too close together shield each other from the water spray inside the dishwasher and are likely to remain soiled when the dishwasher stops. $$$ ●

52 RUN FULL LOADS OF LAUNDRY

It is more cost-effective to wash one full load than two small ones. If you have to run a small load, set the water level appropriately. $$$ ●

53 WASH CLOTHES IN COOLER WATER

Up to 85 percent of the cost of operating a washing machine comes from heating the water. Cut that energy use in half by switching the temperature control from hot to warm. For even greater savings, wash in cold water. Today's cold-water detergents make hot water unnecessary except when dealing with stubborn grease stains. $$$ ●

54 TAKE ADVANTAGE OF YOUR CLOTHES DRYER'S AUTO-DRY CYCLE

Many dryers—gas and electric—have moisture sensors that detect when the clothes are dry and turn off the appliance. This auto-dry feature prevents overdrying your clothes, which not only increases your utility bill unnecessarily, but is rough on clothing as well. $$$ ●

55 IN SUNNY WEATHER, HANG WET LAUNDRY ON A CLOTHESLINE

Letting your clothes air-dry adds absolutely nothing to your utility bills. $$$ ●

56 DRY LIGHTWEIGHT ITEMS SEPARATELY

Socks, underwear, and the like will take less time to dry if you separate them from towels and other water-absorbent items. You save money even though you run the dryer twice. $$$ ●

57 REMOVE CLOTHES FROM THE DRYER PROMPTLY TO MINIMIZE IRONING

Shake your clothes out when they are still warm from the dryer and slightly damp, then hang them up. This simple step eliminates the need to iron most of them, saving time and money. $$$ ●

58 CLEAN THE DRYER LINT FILTER AFTER EVERY LOAD

A clean lint filter permits the hot air to circulate freely and dry clothes faster and thus less expensively. $$$ ●

59 DRY MULTIPLE LOADS BACK-TO-BACK

If you are washing more than one load of clothes, dry them one right after the other to take advantage of the heat already built up in the dryer. $$$ ●

60 REPLACE YOUR OLD CLOTHES WASHER WITH AN EXTRA-EFFICIENT MODEL

The washing machine competes with the refrigerator for the title of top energy-consuming appliance in your home. Over the past several years, however, clothes washers have become significantly more efficient. The best are front-loading models; they use a tumble action to move clothes in and out of less water than top-loading machines require. But there are new, efficient top-loaders as well. All clothes washers bearing the Energy Star label (page 9) cost more but use 35 to 50 percent less water per load than other clothes washers and up to 50 percent less energy.

When shopping for a new clothes washer, look for features that will save you money on every load. They include the option to match water level to the size of the load, and even a minibasket that fits over the agitator to let you wash a few pieces of clothing economically. Additionally, there's a pre-soak cycle that permits a shorter wash time, a high-pressure spray cycle that replaces full-tub rinsing, and a high-speed spin cycle that extracts more water from clean clothes than a regular spin cycle, reducing drying time to save even more money. $$ ●

61 INSPECT THE DRYER EXHAUST VENT REGULARLY

A clogged vent, like a lint-packed filter, reduces dryer efficiency. Check that the vent is clear by feeling for warm, moist air at the exit after the dryer has been operating for several minutes. Also, observe whether the outside flap opens freely to let the hot air out and closes to bar entry to rain and small animals. If not, install a new one (page 49). $$ ●

62 PURCHASE A GAS DRYER

If you are in the market for a new clothes dryer, consider one heated by natural gas or propane (LPG). Either type is considerably less expensive to run than an electrically heated unit. $$ ●

63 INSTALL THE WASHING MACHINE CLOSE TO THE WATER HEATER—OR VICE VERSA

The shorter the distance hot water must travel between the water heater and the washing machine, the less heat is lost through the pipes along the way. $$ ●

64 SET THERMOSTATS HIGHER IN SUMMER, LOWER IN WINTER

In hot weather, each degree that you raise the thermostat setting for air conditioning saves about 2 percent on your cooling bill and lightens the load on the energy grid. Try to acclimate yourself to a setting of 78°F or higher. A fan in the room can make it feel cooler than the thermostat setting, and it costs less to run the fan than it does the air conditioner.

In cool weather, set the thermostat at 68°F or lower for a comparable decrease in your heating expenses. Living within this temperature range can significantly trim your energy bill. $$$ ●

65 DON'T PAY TO HEAT OR COOL AN EMPTY HOUSE

There's no point in heating or cooling an empty house or apartment when you leave home for a weekend or longer. Save money in warm weather by setting your thermostat to 85°F, or simply turn the air conditioning off. In cool weather, set the thermostat to 65°F or lower. Reset or reprogram the thermostat on your arrival home. $$$ ●

66 CLOSE THE REGISTERS OR TURN OFF RADIATORS IN AN UNUSED ROOM

Stopping the flow of heated or cooled air to a room, then shutting the door to isolate it can save 5 to 10 percent of your heating and cooling costs. There are a couple of exceptions, however. Unless you have electric baseboard heating,

with a thermostat in every room, you may not be able to seal off a room fitted with a thermostat. In that case, closing the door often raises or lowers the temperature in other parts of the house controlled by the same thermostat. Also, if you heat your house with a heat pump, closing registers causes a heat pump to run inefficiently and might harm it. $$$ ●

67 TURN OFF EXHAUST FANS AS SOON AS THE NEED FOR THEM PASSES

Exhaust fans excel at extracting heat- and moisture-laden air from kitchens, bathrooms, and laundry rooms. Indeed, they are so effective that, in an hour or two, they can expel a whole houseful of warmed or cooled air. To save energy dollars, run exhaust fans no longer than necessary to do their work. $$ ●

68 OPEN DOORS INSIDE THE HOUSE TO MAXIMIZE HEATING AND COOLING EFFICIENCY

Whenever possible, leave doors between rooms open to assist air circulation. Exceptions are houses with more than one thermostat, such as those with electric baseboard heating or two furnaces and air conditioners that serve different parts of the building. In such cases, close doors that join areas controlled by different thermostats. $$$ ●

69 MOVE HOME FURNISHINGS AND OTHER APPOINTMENTS AWAY FROM FORCED-AIR REGISTERS

For maximum heating and cooling efficiency, don't trap costly heated or cooled air behind sofas, drapes, and similar obstructions. Keep drapes near registers open as much as possible, and re-arrange furniture to promote air circulation. $$$ ●

70 INSTALL A PROGRAMMABLE THERMOSTAT

The multiple settings of a programmable thermostat can cut your heating and cooling costs by up to one-third. These energy-conserving devices connect to existing thermostat wiring (page 62). They can automatically adjust heating and cooling temperatures as many as six times a day, with different profiles for weekdays and weekends.

Program the thermostat to provide a comfortable temperature when you are at home and a more economical temperature when you are away. If you wish, you can temporarily override the program, then revert to it later.

A heat pump requires a special programmable thermostat that raises the setting in several small steps instead of a single big one. This approach minimizes the use of the unit's backup heat source, often costly-to-run electric heating elements. $$ ●

71 PLUG AIR LEAKS THAT RAISE UTILITY BILLS BY LETTING OUTDOOR AIR INTO THE HOUSE

Doors and windows are the most likely sources of air leaks. To find them, wait for a windy day, then slowly move a lighted candle, smoke pencil, or incense stick around window and door frames. Wherever the flame or smoke flutters or drifts, an air leak is the cause. It needs to be closed, caulked, or weather-stripped (page 58).

Less-obvious leaks can occur where plumbing, ducting, and electrical wiring penetrate exterior walls. Using the flame or hanging plastic technique (page 58), check around your electrical service panel (circuit-breaker box), plumbing where it passes through exterior walls, electrical outlets, ductwork, exhaust vents, window-mounted air conditioners, and other places

where outside air might be sneaking into the house. When you find a leak, seal it with caulking, expanding foam, insulation, or a gasket (pages 60–61). $$ ●

72 KEEP HUMIDITY UNDER CONTROL

Because relative humidity affects comfort, tailoring the humidity in your house to the season reduces the use of energy for heating and cooling. For most people, a relative humidity of around 60 percent in winter permits a thermostat setting for heat that would be too low in dryer air. In summer, a relative humidity of 40 percent allows a thermostat setting for air conditioning that would be uncomfortably high in more humid air.

Both air conditioners and furnaces dry the air in your house. In summer, that's usually all right, but in winter and during summers in desertlike climes, the air often becomes too dry. The solution is to install a humidifier at the furnace or to purchase a stand-alone unit. If the air in your house is uncomfortably damp despite heating and air conditioning, consider buying a dehumidifier to pull additional moisture from the air. $$ ●

73 AT LEAST ONCE A MONTH, CHECK THE FILTER IN A FORCED-AIR HEATING AND COOLING SYSTEM

A dirty filter can raise your furnace or air conditioner's energy consumption by 5 to 15 percent. Furnace overheating that can result from a clogged filter can shut down the system completely. Monthly replacement may be necessary even if the manufacturer of the filter you buy advertises that it works much longer than 30 days. The fine mesh of many such filters can actually fill more quickly than that of less-effective ones. To check a filter, simply extract it from its slot near the blower. $$ ●

74 CLEAN YOUR HEATING AND COOLING SYSTEM WHERE IT DELIVERS THE GOODS

Dust on the registers in a forced-air system can cut its efficiency by 10 percent or more. The same goes for dust on baseboard heaters and radiators. Vacuum these parts of your heating system regularly using a brush nozzle. Unscrew registers from walls—floor registers simply lift out—and vacuum accessible surfaces inside the ducts. Use a flexible hose rather than a metal or plastic wand, and fasten the brush securely to the hose with duct tape. $$ ●

75 REMOVE DUST BUILDUP FROM THE BLOWER OF A FORCED-AIR HEATING SYSTEM

Despite the filter in your furnace, the blower that circulates air throughout the house can become caked with dust, reducing its efficiency. Wipe and vacuum dust from the blower blades and the walls of the blower chamber two or three times a year. $$ ●

76 HAVE YOUR DUCTS INSPECTED

About two-thirds of American homes have forced-air heating and air-conditioning systems that circulate warm or cool air through metal ductwork. Damaged ducts and loose joints between duct sections can account for up to 40 percent of a home's energy loss. With the furnace blower running, you can feel or hear air escaping from leaks in exposed sections and fix them yourself. To find leaks under floors and behind ceilings and walls, you can have a heating-and-air-conditioning professional conduct a pressurized test of the ducts and repair any leaks it reveals. $$ ●

77 HAVE YOUR FURNACE AND AIR CONDITIONER SERVICED REGULARLY BY A PRO

Periodic maintenance of your furnace and air conditioner reduces energy costs by 3 to 10 percent. Although you can change filters and clean accessible parts yourself, only qualified professionals can perform the necessary inspection and maintenance of other parts, such as the combustion chamber and refrigerant lines. Schedule a professional checkup once a year for air conditioners and oil-fired furnaces and every 2 years for gas furnaces and heat pumps. $ ●

78 SEAL EXTERIOR WALLS IN NEW CONSTRUCTION OR REMODELING WORK

Eliminate leaks in exterior walls by having your builder both install house wrap and tape or caulk joints in exterior sheathing. A well-sealed building will repay you with savings of up to 30 percent on future heating and cooling bills. $$ ●

80 A LIGHTER OR DARKER ROOF COLOR COULD SAVE YOU MONEY

When the time comes to replace an asphalt-shingle roof, your choice of color can affect your energy bill. In mostly warm, sunny regions, a light-colored roof that reflects heat is the best choice. If you have long, cold winters, consider a dark roof to absorb heat from the sun. The right choice can save up to 10 percent on energy costs. $$ ●

79 REPAINT WITH ENERGY SAVINGS IN MIND

Choosing the right paint color for your exterior walls can play a role in your energy-saving strategy. For example, walls painted or stained a dark tone absorb 70 to 90 percent of radiant energy from the sun, a good choice in regions with harsh winters and mild summers. Lighter colors, which reflect heat, are more suitable for brutally hot summers and moderate winters. $ ●

The Value of Trees

Studies conducted by the Lawrence Berkeley National Laboratory found summer daytime air temperatures to be 3° to 6°F cooler in tree-shaded neighborhoods than in treeless areas. Not only do trees block direct sunlight, but water evaporating from trees helps cool surrounding air.

According to the U.S. Department of Energy, trees that shade the south and southwest sides of a house can cut between $100 and $250 annually from air-conditioning costs. If your property is unshaded, planting the right trees in the right places offers long-term benefits. The height, growth rate, regional adaptability, branch spread, and shape of different tree varieties are all factors to consider in choosing the most beneficial trees.

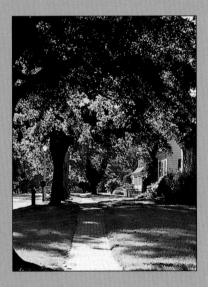

Deciduous trees, which shed leaves in autumn, are preferable where winters are harsh; the leafless trees let in sunlight to help warm the house. In subtropical or desert areas, evergreen trees that shade the house all year are best.

81 SHELTER YOUR HOUSE FROM WINDS THAT COOL IT IN WINTER AND WARM IT IN SUMMER

Windbreaks on the north and west sides of a house reduce the chilling effect of cold winter winds. Similarly, planting windbreaks on the south and west sides of a house can help deflect hot summer winds that tend to pull cooler air from inside. Evergreen trees and tall shrubs planted close together make the best windbreaks, but even vines grown on trellises help to deflect wind around windows, which are the most poorly insulated parts of a house. $ ●

82 STOP COOLING YOUR LIGHT BULBS

When the air conditioning is on, turning off as many lights as is practical can help trim your cooling bill. Incandescent light bulbs give off a surprising amount of heat. In an hour, for example, ten 100-watt bulbs put out more than 3,000 BTUs (British Thermal Units) of heat. That's more than 6 percent of the cooling capacity of a 4-ton air conditioner, which is big enough to cool a moderate-size house. $$$ ●

83 SCHEDULE HEAT-PRODUCING CHORES FOR COOLER PARTS OF THE DAY

In hot weather, do housework such as cooking, clothes drying, and ironing early in the morning or after sunset when the ambient temperature is lower. Your air conditioner will not have to work so hard, and the savings go straight to your energy bill. $$$ ●

84 KEEP SOURCES OF HEAT AWAY FROM YOUR THERMOSTAT

A lamp or even a TV set placed near a thermostat can waste valuable energy by fooling this sensitive instrument into concluding that the temperature inside your entire house is what the thermostat is sensing. As a result, the thermostat turns on the air conditioner unnecessarily. To avoid this, keep incandescent lamps and other electric appliances at least 4 feet from the thermostat. $$$ ●

85 DISPERSE SUMMER HEAT BUILDUP AROUND YOUR HOUSE WITH A SPRINKLER

At dusk on a hot summer day, water the lawn and paved areas around your house. Cooling these surfaces prevents them from radiating, for hours after sunset, heat absorbed during the day. That in turn reduces the evening heat load on your house and can trim your air-conditioning bill. $$ ●

86 SHADE WINDOWS FROM SUMMER SUN

From May to September in many climates, sunny rooms are hot rooms. Drapes and blinds can confine some of the heat next to the windows, but the best defense is to block the sun before it reaches the windows, before the greenhouse effect can take over.

Trees planted to shade the southern and western windows are effective barriers to sunlight, but they require years of growth to become fully effective. Results can be had sooner by installing awnings or shade trellises. Either solution can keep sun out in summer and let it in during winter. Another option is to install shade cloth outside your windows. This material can weaken sunlight by 90 percent, yet allows a breeze to pass. It comes as roller blinds ready for installation, or in bulk for stretching across frames. $$$ ●

87 HANG A FAN FROM THE CEILING

Overhead fans with variable speeds, reversible rotation, and variable-pitch blades optimize heating and cooling, especially in rooms with high ceilings. Most fans replace a light fixture, whose anchorage in the ceiling may need strengthening to support the often substantial weight of a ceiling fan (page 67).

In summer, use the fan to lift cool air toward the ceiling from the floor. This approach is especially helpful in rooms cooled by window units or floor registers in a central air-conditioning system. Reversing the fan in winter helps circulate warm air trapped against the ceiling. $ ●

88 SUBSTITUTE WATT-SIPPING FANS FOR THAT KILOWATT-GUZZLING AIR CONDITIONER

When you want to feel comfortable indoors without cooling the entire house, an old-fashioned electric fan can be an energy-saving alternative to air-conditioning. The breeze from a fan can make you feel 6°F cooler than the temperature a thermometer shows, while using only a fraction of the electricity consumed by an air conditioner. $$ ●

89 ADD A FAN FOR COOLING THE ENTIRE HOUSE

Typically installed in an attic or vented through the roof, a whole-house fan exhausts warm air trapped in the house and pulls in cooler, outside air through the windows. This kind of ventilation is most effective at night or early in the morning, when outside air is more likely to be cooler than inside air. The fan housing should be well insulated. Most have louvers that close automatically to block outside air when you turn the fan off. $$$ ●

90 COOL SEVERAL ROOMS WITH A BOX FAN

On mild days or overnight, place a box fan in an open window so that it exhausts warm air from the house, drawing in cooler air through other open windows. Using fans in this way during periods of warm days and cool nights can reduce energy used for cooling by 60 percent or more compared with the cost of running your air conditioner. Over the long haul, your savings on electricity will far outweigh the cost of the fan. $$ ●

91 RESIST SETTING THE AIR CONDITIONER THERMOSTAT LOWER THAN USUAL TO COOL YOUR HOUSE QUICKLY

If you adjust your air conditioner thermostat to a higher temperature while you're out of the house during the day, you may be tempted upon returning to lower the thermostat setting to an uncomfortably cold temperature in the hope of cooling your house more quickly. This tactic doesn't work. Because an air conditioner cools at maximum output whenever it is running, a colder initial setting does not cool your home any faster. It's more likely to result in excessive cooling and unnecessary expense. $$ ●

92 CLEAN YOUR AIR CONDITIONER'S EVAPORATOR COIL

Dust acts as an insulator for cold as well as for heat. By periodically vacuuming or wiping dust from the evaporator, you improve the coil's efficiency, and that can lead to lower electric bills. $$ ●

93 SHIELD YOUR AIR CONDITIONER FROM THE SUN

An air conditioner running in the shade uses as much as 10 percent less electricity than it would consume in the sun. If possible, put the air conditioner's outdoor heat exchanger, called the condenser, on your home's shadiest side. If you plant trees and shrubs to keep your air conditioner cool, take care not to block the flow of air to the condenser. $$ ●

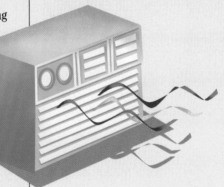

94 MATCH THE AIR CONDITIONER TO THE ROOM

Choosing an air conditioner of the correct capacity for a room assures that you get the most from your energy dollar. Select a unit according to the total area to be cooled.

Air-conditioning capacity, a form of refrigeration, is measured either in British Thermal Units (BTUs) per hour or in tons. (A ton of refrig-

eration absorbs in 24 hours a quantity of heat that would melt 2,000 pounds of ice, about 240,000 BTUs.) A 1-ton unit is comparable to one rated at 10,000 BTUs per hour. As shown in the chart below, such an air conditioner is sufficient to cool a space of 400 to 450 square feet. $$$ ●

Choosing the Right Air Conditioner	
Room Area (Sq. ft.)	Capacity (BTUs/Hour)
100 to 150	5,000
150 to 250	6,000
250 to 350	7,000
350 to 400	9,000
400 to 450	10,000
450 to 550	12,000
550 to 700	14,000
700 to 1,000	18,000

95 VENT THE ATTIC

A ridge vent installed along the roof peak lets hot air escape from the attic while cooler air is drawn in through air vents in the eaves or soffits. This is a job for a professional roofer, but the overall energy savings may well offset the expense. $ ●

How to Buy Heating-and-Cooling Equipment

When it's time to replace your furnace or air conditioner, make energy efficiency a priority. Your exact needs will depend on many factors, among them building design, type of construction, insulation level, orientation on the property, landscaping, and intended use of the system.

Begin with a written calculation of your home's energy needs from a qualified heating and air conditioning professional. Obtain several competitive bids. When ordering new equipment, look for Energy Star and Energy Guide labels (see pages 9 and 11) as indicators of efficiency. Ask about energy fact sheets for the energy-saving potential of different types, models, and sizes of equipment.

96 LET THE WINTER SUN SHINE IN

On cold, clear days, sunlight streaming through a window can warm a room substantially, especially on the southern exposure of your house. The bigger and more numerous the windows, the greater the effect. On cloudy days or when the sun goes down, close the curtains or shades to retain the room's heat. Passive solar heating through windows can reduce heating costs in most houses by 15 to 30 percent. A structure designed to maximize solar effects can enjoy up to 50-percent energy savings over conventional designs. When building or renovating your house, discuss passive solar heating with your architect or builder. The conversation could save you money. $$$ ●

97 ADD A REFLECTIVE SURFACE TO WALLS BEHIND RADIATORS

If your house has radiators or baseboard convectors fed by hot water or steam, you can increase heating efficiency by taping sheets of aluminum foil or foil-covered illustration board to the wall behind each of them. The foil prevents heat from being absorbed by the wall and reflects it into the room. Don't use this technique with electric baseboard heat; it may create a shock hazard. $$$ ●

98 RELEASE TRAPPED AIR FROM RADIATORS AND CONVECTORS

Steam and hot-water heating systems lose effectiveness when air pockets develop in the radiators or convectors. Bleed air from these components at the beginning of each heating season and whenever you hear the telltale knocking produced by air lodged in the system. $$$ ●

99 SLOW THE ESCAPE OF HEAT THROUGH THE GLASS IN WINDOWS AND DOORS

If you live in a region with cold winters—and your home has large expanses of glass—hang insulating curtains or draperies in front of windows and glass doors to reduce heat loss, especially at night. $$ ●

100 HELP COOL YOUR HOUSE WITH SKYLIGHTS

If your house has a room with a cathedral ceiling or a finished attic without air conditioning, consider installing skylights that

open and close. They can serve as vents to expel warm air during the summer.

Skylights should be double-glazed, preferably with low-E glass (see page 28). Motorized skylights come with a remote control and a rain sensor to shut them automatically at the first sprinkle. Some manually operated skylights can be fitted with a motor and rain sensor. $ ●

101 CLOSE THE FIREPLACE DAMPER

Leaving a fireplace damper open is like keeping a window wide open day and night and can account for 5 to 15 percent of your total energy cost for heating. Close the damper when the fireplace is not in use, and seal openings around the firebox and hearth with caulking material specially formulated for use in fireplaces. $$$ ●

102 MAKE YOUR WOOD-BURNING FIREPLACE A BETTER SOURCE OF HEAT

Invest in a fireplace grate made of several C-shaped metal tubes arranged side-by-side so that their ends point into the room. As the fire heats the grate, cool air is drawn from the room into the lower ends of the tubes, then warmed and returned to the room from the upper ends. Other grates hold logs in a way that increases the heat radiated into the room. $$ ●

103 CONVERT YOUR FIREPLACE FROM A WOOD-BURNER TO A GAS-BURNER

A pre-fabricated metal fireplace or fireplace insert that burns natural gas or propane offers an energy-saving option to a conventional fire-

place. Most models are designed to look like log fires, and some can be installed in the middle of a room rather than against a wall. Gas-burning units are vented to use outside air for combustion and to expel burned gases through ducts if the house has no chimney.

A gas-fed fireplace burns more evenly than a wood-fueled unit and its heat output is more easily controlled. A zero-clearance firebox is designed to be installed close to wood or dry-wall without the need for a masonry hearth and chimney. In the long run, your energy savings should more than offset the installation costs of venting and running gas lines. $ ●

104 LESSEN THE CHILLING EFFECT OF A ROARING FIRE

Each hour, a fire in your fireplace can pull as much as 24,000 cubic feet of air out of your house and up the chimney, replacing it with air from outdoors. Warming this chilly influx puts a huge strain on your heating budget. You can minimize this heat loss by closing the doors to the room with the fireplace and opening a window an inch or so. This gives the fire all the fresh air it needs and prevents it from drawing warm air from other rooms. $$$ ●

105 INSTALL A FIREPLACE ENCLOSURE

You can get more heat from your fireplace if you install a glass-and-metal fireplace enclosure. Many models have a heat exchanger with a fan that blows warmed air into the room when a fire is burning. Their tempered glass doors seal off the fireplace when it's not in use to help the damper keep warm air in the house. $ ●

106 INSTALL RADIANT HEAT

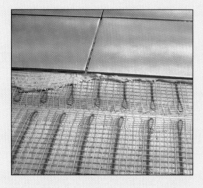

A house built on a slab can benefit from a radiant heat system that circulates hot water through tubing embedded in the concrete. Radiant heat can be up to 40 percent more energy efficient than forced-air heat. Beyond that, radiant heat makes the floor feel pleasantly warm to bare feet. This type of heating lends itself to zoning, so that each room can have its own thermostat. The hot water source can be a boiler, water heater, heat pump, or an energy-saving solar collector.

In recent years, electric radiant heat systems (left, below) have also come into their own. Relying on slender cables or flat panels of conductive material to produce the heat, they layer on the floor without thickening it more than an inch. These systems are relatively easy to install, although a licensed electrician should make all the connections. Usually the cables are placed in a bed of mortar and covered with tile, natural stone, wood, vinyl, or carpeting. $$ ●

107 UPGRADE TO PELLETS

Pellet stoves and furnaces are cleaner burning, more powerful, more energy efficient—and more expensive—than the best wood stoves. Their fuel is recycled sawdust and other organic material compressed into small pellets that are loaded into a bin and automatically fed into the combustion chamber as needed. Pellet stoves can produce more than enough heat for a large room or living area. As with a wood stove, check local codes and have an expert evaluate your heating needs before buying.

When your furnace bites the dust, consider replacing it with one fueled by pellets. Such a furnace can generate up to 100,000 BTUs an hour, enough to heat a good-size house. $$ ●

108 WHERE FIREWOOD COSTS LITTLE OR NOTHING, CONSIDER A WOOD-BURNING STOVE TO CUT HEATING COSTS

Old-fashioned cast-iron wood stoves are woefully inefficient, sending 40 to 80 percent of the heat up the chimney and polluting the atmosphere as well. But a modern wood stove—with a catalytic converter to limit pollution, a secondary combustion chamber to burn smoke and gases that would otherwise go up the chimney, and a blower to circulate the warm air it produces—is a different matter.

These stoves burn less wood more cleanly to generate a greater quantity of heat than their predecessors. Wood stoves vary widely in design, heat output, and efficiency, as do local codes governing their use. It pays to have an expert evaluate your home and heating needs before making a purchase. $$ ●

How Much Insulation Is Enough?

The insulation industry rates the resistance to heat flow of its products with a system of R-values; the greater the R-value, the harder it is for heat to get through. Higher R-values are recommended for some parts of the house than for others. For example, exterior walls should be insulated to at least R-11. Floors over unheated spaces should be at least R-19. Ceilings below a roof or attic should be R-30 or higher. R-values are additive. So, if you find, say, R-19 in your attic, you can add insulation rated at R-11 to bring the total value to R-30. The climate map on page 70 shows recommended R-values for homes within each zone. The higher the zone number, the greater the recommended R-value for a particular use.

Insulating batts, rolls, and boards are labeled with their R-value. The R-value of loose material, which varies with thickness, is available from the manufacturer or installer.

109 STOP HEAT THEFT BY RECESSED LIGHTING

Light fixtures set into an upstairs ceiling often waste heat by leaking it into the attic. To prevent this

loss, you can insulate the fixtures from above, although doing so may be practical only in an attic without a floor. Before proceeding, confirm that the fixture label is marked designed for direct insulation contact. You can lay insulation right up against such fixtures. With units that are not rated, this technique creates a fire hazard. Insulate them as shown on page 72. $ ●

110 IF YOUR HOUSE HAS A CRAWL SPACE OR AN UNFINISHED BASEMENT, INSULATE IT

Although heat rises, it also escapes downward through the floor above an uninsulated crawl space or basement. Install insulation between the joists that support the ground floor. In addition, wrap insulation around any heating ducts that pass through the crawl space. If your furnace is in the basement, insulate the walls to retain heat radiated

by the furnace (pages 76–77). Doing so warms the floor above the basement and both warms and dries the basement itself, improving its utility as storage space.
$$ ●

111 ADD INSULATION TO AN UNFINISHED ATTIC

The best and easiest place to lower your heating and cooling bill with insulation is an unfinished attic, either between ceiling joists or between the rafters directly against the roof. Or you can lay additional insulation across joists and rafters if the spaces between them are already full. To judge whether you need more insulation in your attic, measure the thickness of any insulation you find there. If you discover less than 6 inches of fiberglass or 5 inches of loose cellulose, the insulation value is below R-19. It's time to add more (page 71). $$ ●

112 UPGRADE INSULATION IN EXTERIOR WALLS

Checking insulation within exterior walls or above a ceiling in a finished attic presents obvious problems. If R-values are not available from the builder, you can get a sense of the situation by removing electrical-outlet cover plates and plumbing access panels—as well as heating and cooling registers—to gain limited access to the interior of a wall. In finished areas, bringing insulation up to recommended R-values can be an expensive measure that usually requires a contractor. But future energy savings may justify the cost if you live in a very hot or very cold climate. $ ●

113 RESTORE DETERIORATED INSULATION TO FULL EFFECTIVENESS

Discolored or damaged spots on exposed insulation, especially near corners and edges of the roof or ceilings, may indicate air and moisture leaks. These openings can be difficult to find, and repairing them may require replacing a section of roofing or siding, or other jobs perhaps best left to a carpenter or roofer. Inside, seal holes by patching the damage or by caulking visible cracks. Only when the house is weather tight again should you replace any damaged insulation. $$ ●

Advantages of Low-E Glass

Ordinary window glass is an excellent conductor of heat, permitting more heat energy to enter and escape from the house than do the walls and roof. So, the more windows in a house, the more it can benefit from low-E glass (E stands for emissivity), which is a better heat barrier than a common windowpane.

Low-E glass has a transparent, heat-reflective coating that helps minimize heating and cooling costs. In summer, low-E glass deflects heat from the sun that would otherwise warm the interior of a house. In winter, it reflects back into the house warmth generated by your heating system.

114 ADD AN INSULATING LAYER OF AIR WITH STORM WINDOWS

Creating a dead-air space next to house windows significantly increases the R-value of any windowpane, especially the single-glazed variety. Installing storm windows also reduces drafts, condensation, and frost formation, all of which steal heat from the house. The wider the air space, the better the thermal insulation. A ¾-inch gap is the recommended minimum; one of several inches is more effective. Consult a window supplier for advice on how best to find storm windows that fit the windows in your house. $ ●

115 INSTALL PLASTIC FILM INSTEAD OF STORM WINDOWS

For a less costly and less permanent alternative to storm windows outdoors, cover your windows with clear plastic sheeting indoors (page 54). $$ ●

116 USE STORM DOORS YEAR-ROUND

Where air-conditioning is needed even at night, it makes good sense to dispense with traditional screen doors in favor of solid entry doors or storm doors even in summer. The greater insulation value of storm doors or entry doors with high U-values will help to retain cooled air, whereas a screen door lets it escape. $$ ●

U-Values for Doors and Windows

Framed window and door units are rated with a numerical U-value that indicates their relative heat conductivity. Look for U-value labels on new window and door installations. A low U-value is desirable for reflecting the sun's heat in summer and reducing heat loss in winter. U-values range from a high of 0.7 for ordinary glass to a low of 0.22 in the most energy-efficient units.

117 WHEN REMODELING OR EXPANDING YOUR HOUSE, CHOOSE WINDOWS THAT LOWER UTILITY BILLS

For maximum energy savings, buy gas-filled, double-pane units made with low-E glass. Because there are so many window options available, consult a knowledgeable contractor or window manufacturer to select the most energy-efficient, cost-effective windows and glass doors for your region. $$ ●

118 CLOSE THE DOOR TO ENERGY WASTE WITH A HIGH-U REPLACEMENT

An old-style entry door, especially one with a large expanse of ordinary single-pane window glass, can be a significant source of energy loss. Pre-framed exterior door units designed and built to a high U-value can help save money. Look for wood, fiberglass-, or steel-clad door units featuring insulation built into the door panel and low-E glass. $ ●

119 PLUG THE BASIN DRAIN WHEN WASHING UP OR SHAVING

You can save a gallon of hot water each time you wash your hands and face or shave if you close the wash-basin drain and run only the hot water you need. Empty the basin when you're finished soaping and refill with warm water for a quick rinse. The hot water savings can add up to 50 or more gallons per person every month. For a family of four, that comes to about 2,500 gallons a year. $$$ ●

120 SHOWER, DON'T BATHE

A bathtub half-full of hot water holds at least 10 gallons more than the 15 gallons you use for a 5-minute shower. A family of four showering daily instead of bathing can save the cost of heating as much as 200 gallons of water every week. $$$ ●

121 TAKE SHORTER SHOWERS

Every minute that you trim from a shower saves the cost of heating about 3 gallons of water. For real economy, take a "Navy shower." Wet yourself and a washcloth thoroughly, then turn off the water while you shampoo and lather yourself clean. Turn on the water again to rinse. $$$ ●

122 TURN THE KITCHEN FAUCET TO COLD

When using small amounts of water, keep the lever on the kitchen faucet set to COLD, especially when hot water has not recently made the trip from the heater to the faucet. In this situation, moving the lever to HOT lets hot water enter the supply line even though the hot water never reaches the faucet, and the water heater must warm the cold water that replenishes the tank. $$$ ●

123 DON'T HEAT WATER UNNECESSARILY IF YOU'RE OUT OF TOWN

Whenever you leave home for a weekend or longer, there's no point in heating water that no one will use. Either set the water-heater thermostat to its lowest setting or turn off the water heater altogether. Reset the thermostat as soon as you return; you'll have hot water again in an hour. $$$ ●

124 SAVE MONEY WITH THE WATER HEATER BUILT INTO YOUR DISHWASHER

The appliance that typically requires the hottest water in the house is the dishwasher at 140°F. If your dishwasher has its own built-in heater—and most modern dishwashers do—you can reset the household water-heater thermostat to 120°F. Heat controls on water heaters are often inaccurate, so measure the temperature with a cooking thermometer and adjust the thermostat as necessary.

This idea won't work if you have a water heater that's too small for your requirements. Then it will pay to keep the water temperature higher, lowering it with cold water as needed for laundry, showers, and washing dishes. $$$ ●

125 RELY MORE ON YOUR DISHWASHER TO SAVE HOT WATER

Not only do automatic dishwashers clean dishes and flatware more thoroughly than hand washing, they can save 6 or more gallons of hot water per load compared with washing the same dishes by hand. If you run the dishwasher once a day, you save the cost of heating more than 2,000 gallons of hot water a year. $$$ ●

126 BUY AN ELECTRIC KETTLE

If you frequently boil water in a kettle on an electric stove, consider using an efficient electric kettle instead. Because the heating element is dedicated to the kettle, less heat is lost, and your water will boil sooner. $ ●

127 INSULATE THE WATER HEATER

If your heater feels hot or even merely warm to the touch, it's wasting energy through heat transfer. Although modern ceramic- or glass-lined heaters have some built-in insulation, you can decrease heat loss by wrapping a closely fitting insulation blanket around the water heater (page 80). $$ ●

128 REPAIR LEAKY FAUCETS

A hot-water valve that leaks just one drop per second can waste as much as 400 gallons of heated water a year. The cost of that wasted water ends up on your utility bill. Repairing leaky faucets is a cheap way to save both money and energy, especially if you do the work yourself (pages 84–89). $$$ ●

129 FLUSH SEDIMENT FROM THE BOTTOM OF THE WATER TANK

When water is heated, calcium carbonate dissolved in the water becomes un-dissolved. The resulting precipitate settles to the bottom of the water tank, where it impedes heat transfer—especially in gas-fired units because the heat source is under the tank. To clear sediment buildup, drain several gallons of water from the tank at least twice a year—more often if you have very hard water (page 82). $$ ●

130 INSULATE HOT-WATER LINES

Wherever your hot-water pipes are accessible, fight heat loss by covering them with slip-on pipe insulation or with fiberglass or foil-backed insulation made for wrapping around pipes (page 79). You'll find this material, made of foam or fiberglass, in convenient lengths at any home center. $$ ●

131 INSTALL LOW-FLOW FAUCET AERATORS

Faucet aerators mix air with the stream of water to reduce volume without significantly lowering pressure. Low-flow models available for the bathroom limit volume to as little as 1 gallon per minute. Similar aerators for the kitchen are typically set for 2½ gallons per minute. Replacing your present aerator with a low-flow model takes about 5 minutes (page 82). $$ ●

132 REPLACE OLD SHOWERHEADS WITH NEWER, LOW-FLOW MODELS

For new homes, plumbing codes now require showerheads that deliver no more than 2½ gallons of water per minute, enough for an adequate spray. Low-flow showerheads can save a typical family of four around 15,000 gallons of hot water a year.

That comes to about $75 annually if you heat water with gas, $150 if you have an electric water heater. You save even more if you live where energy prices are high. These simple devices can pay for themselves in about a month, especially if you install them yourself (page 82). $$ ●

133 INSTALL A HIGH-EFFICIENCY WATER HEATER

When the time comes to replace your water heater, select a new one with energy efficiency in mind. Electric water heaters are generally more expensive to run. If natural or bottled gas is readily available, a gas-fired heater can save up to 50 percent over the cost of heating water with electricity.

When shopping, look for the Energy Guide label (page 11) and ask the advice of your appliance dealer or utility company. Both can help you choose the most efficient unit that will satisfy your family's hot-water needs. $ ●

134 PUT AN INSTANT WATER HEATER IN YOUR KITCHEN

If you often need small amounts of hot water for cooking or washing, consider installing an instant heater next to the kitchen sink (page 90). Because it eliminates the need to run hot water through the entire supply line, this compact, electrically powered unit is especially economical if your kitchen is some distance from the main water heater. $ ●

135 CONVERT TO A TANKLESS WATER HEATING SYSTEM

When replacing your water heater, consider a tankless system, which heats water on demand instead of storing many gallons of it at the ready. Smaller units can serve a bathroom or kitchen; larger units are capable of supplying hot water to an entire dwelling.

When a hot-water valve is opened, a tankless unit instantly heats the water flowing through it at rates up to 3 gallons per minute. Because water is heated only when it is needed, a tankless system can cut water-heating costs by as much as 60 percent over the long term, even though it costs more to buy than a conventional heater.

Tankless heaters are ideally suited to small apartments or condominiums. In a house with multiple bathrooms, even a large-capacity system may falter when asked to supply hot water for a couple of showers, plus the dishwasher and clothes washer—all at the same time. One solution is to stagger hot-water demand. Another is to install a smaller unit near each point of use. $ ●

136 HARNESS THE SUN TO HEAT YOUR WATER

If you live in a sunny clime, especially in a region where there is little freezing weather, you'll save on energy costs by installing a simple solar hot-water collector or water heater to supplement a conventional water heater (page 91).

The Florida Solar Energy Commission estimates that over an extended period of time, one of these relatively inexpensive solar hot-water sources is 50- to 85-percent less expensive to operate than an electric water heater. The savings over gas water heaters are less substantial and may not be cost-effective for most homeowners. More sophisticated systems, costing thousands of dollars for materials and professional installation, typically take years to pay for themselves through lowered costs for hot water. $ ●

MONEY-SAVING PROJECTS YOU CAN DO YOURSELF

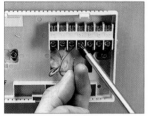

Even after you and your family have become accustomed to saving energy by routinely turning off unneeded lights, taking shorter hot showers, and making minor concessions on room temperature, you have yet to tap a rich source of cost-shaving measures. The next steps you can take require only a few basic tools and a modest investment of time and energy.

In the pages that follow, you will learn how to repair leaky faucets that needlessly add to your water and water-heating bills. There are also simple steps for cleaning coils on your refrigerator so it can cool better with less electricity, for sealing your house against hot and cold air leaks, for adding insulation where your house needs more, and making other proven, energy-saving repairs and improvements.

Of course, you can always call in a plumber to fix that faucet, a heating and cooling technician to install an improved thermostat, or specialists to boost your home's insulation. But the expense of doing so will push back the day when those improvements pay for themselves. It's far more economical to do the work yourself, and you can put the money saved toward other improvements that will help cut your energy needs even further.

SAVING MONEY ON LIGHTING

You can achieve a noticeable reduction in your electric bill simply by summoning the discipline to turn off lights in unoccupied rooms, taking better advantage of natural light for daytime activities, and following other simple energy-conserving guidelines.

To save additional energy—and lower your power bill accordingly—may require further action to improve the electrical efficiency of your home. Some measures involve no more than screwing a different kind of bulb into your lamps and light

fixtures or switching to night-lights that barely disturb your electric meter (below).

Other energy-saving options call for disconnecting some of the switches and light fixtures in your house in order to replace them with alternatives such as dimmer switches and fluorescent fixtures that can save you money in the long run—or even the short run if you can avoid the expense of an electrician.

The electrical work described on the following pages is largely a matter of loosening and tightening a few screws and splicing wires together in the same arrangement that greets you when you remove the cover plate from an electrical box. Usually, black wires connect to black wires, white to white, and green to green or to a bare wire. Occasionally, you may encounter a connection between a black and a red wire. All the work is safe if you always turn off power to the circuit that you're about to work on, as described on the facing page.

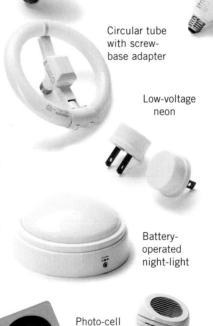

Compact fluorescent bulbs

Circular tube with screw-base adapter

Low-voltage neon

Battery-operated night-light

Photo-cell lights

Economical Replacement Bulbs

You can save money on lighting simply by giving up incandescent bulbs in favor of fluorescent replacements, which emit about four times as much light as an incandescent bulb of the same wattage. Called compact fluorescent lamps (CFLs), they screw into standard light fixtures and come in a variety of shapes and sizes to fit almost any lamp. Some resemble an ordinary light bulb; others have tubes bent into the shape of a U or a coil. CFLs may not fit in some ceiling fixtures. For them, an adapter is available that screws into the light bulb socket and accepts a circular fluorescent tube. The adapter is suitable for any ceiling fixture that's big enough to accept it.

Energy-Saving Night-Lights

At its worst, a night-light consumes only a few watts performing its nightly duty of comforting children who wake before morning and aiding nighttime navigation through a darkened house. A battery-powered "moonlight" turns on when you slap the globe, so there's no fumbling in the dark for a switch. Plug-in neon night-lights that glow in a variety of colors and electroluminescent panels that gleam with a bluish tint consume the merest trickle of electricity. Another light that plugs into the wall has a photo sensor that turns the light on automatically at night. In addition, the light pivots so that you can aim it along a hallway.

Working Safely with Electricity

The following pages describe easy ways to install energy-efficient replacement switches and fixtures. These are simple projects that take no more than an hour or two. Furthermore, they are safe if you always take two precautions to prevent electrical shock. First, shut off power to the circuit you will be working on. Second, test to make sure that you have turned the power off as you intended. If you can't confirm that the power is off—or if your wiring doesn't resemble the illustrations that accompany the instructions—call in a professional electrician for advice.

Shutting Off Power

Find your service panel, usually a gray, rectangular box located not far from where electric cables enter the house. Open the panel door; behind it you'll find either circuit breakers or fuses. They control all the electrical circuits in the house.

On the back of the door, there may be an index that tells which outlets or lights are controlled by each breaker or fuse. If you have an index that is accurate, it's easy to find the circuit breaker or fuse you're looking for. Where there's no index, you'll have to experiment: Have a helper turn on a light in the room where you plan to work and shout out when the light goes out as you turn off circuits one by one.

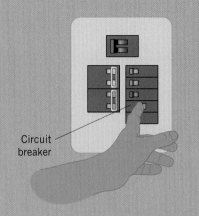

Circuit breaker

To turn off a circuit breaker, flip the toggle switch (above) or push a button, depending on the model. Do not touch any wires in the service panel.

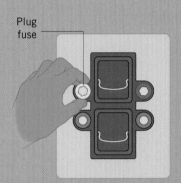

Plug fuse

To shut off a circuit controlled by a fuse, unscrew it completely, and set it aside (above). Place a "Keep Out" sign on the panel door and lock it if possible to ensure that no one will restore power while you work.

Testing for Power

Purchase a voltage tester, which has two probes connected to a small light bulb. To make sure it works, insert the probes into an outlet that's not supplied by the circuit you've turned off. If the tester glows, it's working; use it to check for power at the fixture that you'll be working on.

To do so, remove any cover plate you find, then unscrew the switch or fixture. Pull it from the wall, and unscrew any wire nuts. Don't touch any of the wire ends, and keep them all separated from each other and the electrical box. Next, touch one tester probe to the bare end of a black wire in the box, as you touch the other probe to each white or bare copper wire in the box and to the electrical box itself if it's metal. Repeat the process for each black or red wire in the box. (A red wire is often a sign that two circuits run to the box, requiring that you kill both of them before continuing.) If the tester light glows at any point in the procedure, power to the box is still on. Return to the service panel and try again.

INSTALLING FLUORESCENT FIXTURES

Usually, you can simply remove the mounting hardware for the old fixture from the ceiling box and substitute a strap for the new one. If you encounter hardware different from that shown in the photographs, you can buy any pieces you need at a home center or hardware store.

Removing an Old Fixture

1 Loosening the Screws
After turning off the power (page 35), loosen the screws and lower the fixture past the screw heads. If the fixture mounting holes are too narrow for the screw heads to pass, remove the screws entirely.

2 Disconnecting the Wires
If the fixture's leads are attached to house wires with plastic wire nuts, unscrew them, and pull the wires apart. For leads spliced with electrical tape, snip the house wires as near the splice as you can.

Basic Wirecraft

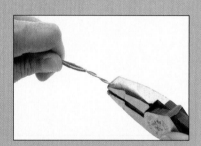

Removing Insulation
To strip a fixture lead, insert the wire about 1 inch into the correct hole of a wire stripper—usually "16" for leads and "14" for house wires. Squeeze the handles, twist, and slide off the insulation. If house wires are long enough, trim the copper ends and re-strip.

Splicing Two Solid Wires
Hold the stripped ends of the two wires side by side and twist them together clockwise at least two turns with linesman's pliers. Snip off the ends of the wires, and screw on a wire nut.

Hanging the New Fixture

Remove the cover from the canopy to expose the fixture wiring, then make any connections within the fixture required by the manufacturer. Long fixtures like the one shown here require more support than an electrical box can offer.

With a stud finder, locate ceiling joists to which the fixture can be fastened, or plan to attach the fixture to the drywall with toggle bolts. Place a drill and screws within easy reach, and arrange for a helper to support the fixture while you work.

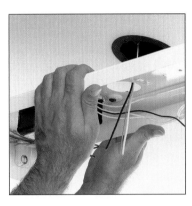

1 Feeding Wires into the Fixture
Remove a knockout in the fixture canopy, then guide the house wires through the knockout hole and position the fixture canopy against the ceiling, so it covers the electrical box.

2 Fastening the Fixture to the Ceiling
If you're mounting the fixture so that it crosses ceiling joists, drill screw holes through the canopy into the joists. When mounting a fixture parallel to the joists, drill holes for toggle bolts through the canopy and the drywall or plaster.

3 Making the Connections
Splice the fixture leads to the house wires, white to white and black to black. If there is a bare house wire or one with green insulation, wrap it around the canopy's green grounding screw, and tighten the screw.

4 Completing the Job
Fold the wires against the canopy, and re-attach the cover, then install the fluorescent tubes. Restore power, and turn on the light. If it doesn't work, try repositioning each tube in its socket. Turn off the light, and snap the plastic diffusing panel into place.

DIMMER SWITCHES

Turning down a dimmer switch decreases the electricity delivered to a fixture, making it more energy efficient. For ceiling fans, use only fan-rated dimmers. If you have a three-way setup—with a light controlled by two switches that do not have ON and OFF printed on their toggles—only one of the switches can be a dimmer. If a single switch controls the ixture, purchase a "single-pole" dimmer.

Can I Install This Switch Here?

A switch box may contain one cable (below, top) or two (below, bottom). Some switches, such as dimmers and programmables, can be installed whether there is one cable or two. Other types—most timers, for instance—can be installed only if two cables enter the box.

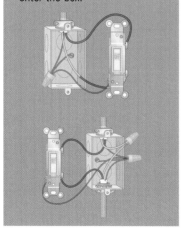

1 Removing the Old Switch

Shut off power to the circuit. Remove the switch cover plate, loosen the old switch's mounting screws, and pull the switch gently out of the wall. Confirm that the power is off (page 35). If the house wires are very short, loosen the terminal screws, and take the wires off the switch to remove it. Snip longer house wires as close to the switch as possible.

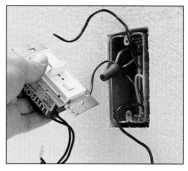

2 Connecting the Ground Wires

If the dimmer has a green grounding lead—many do not—connect it to the bare or green ground wire in the box. In a metal box, you may find the house ground wire screwed to the box. Unscrew it, and connect it to the dimmer's ground lead and to another 6-inch length of bare wire. Screw the other end of this wire to the box.

3 Splicing the Hot and Neutral Wires

Straighten the ends of the black wires. If either breaks, cut off both and strip about 1 inch of insulation from the end of each wire. Splice the switch leads to the house wires (page 36).

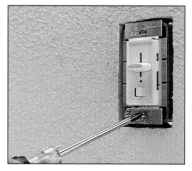

4 Securing the Switch

Fold the house wires and switch leads into the electrical box, then fasten the switch to the box with its two mounting screws so that it's vertical. Attach the cover plate and restore power to the circuit.

Installing a Lamp Dimmer

A number of devices convert an ordinary lamp into one that dims. You can plug a table lamp or a floor lamp into a dimmer that in turn plugs into a wall outlet. Or you can screw a light bulb into a lamp-base dimmer, then screw the assembly into a lamp's light bulb socket. With a little more work, you can add an in-line dimmer to a lamp cord as follows.

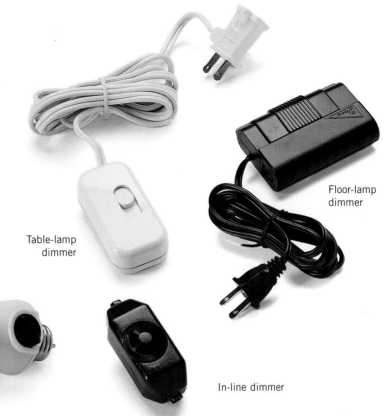

Floor-lamp dimmer

Table-lamp dimmer

Lamp-base dimmer

In-line dimmer

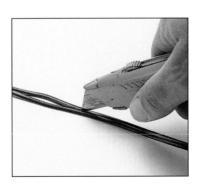

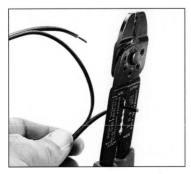

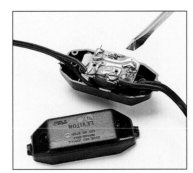

1 **Cutting the Hot Wire**
Unplug the lamp. Separate the cord's two wires with a utility knife as shown above. Examine both wires. The insulation on the neutral wire is ribbed; on the hot wire it's smooth. Cut through the hot wire in the middle of the slit.

2 **Stripping the Hot Wire Ends**
With wire strippers (page 36), remove the insulation from both ends of the cut wire.

3 **Making the Connections**
Remove the switch's cover. Thread the uncut wire through the switch body as shown above. Insert each stripped wire end under a terminal clamp, and tighten the clamp screws. Re-attach the cover, tucking the lamp cord into the opening at each end of the dimmer.

TIMER SWITCHES

A switch with a clock inside saves expensive electricity either by turning off lights, fans, or heating units after a specific length of time or by turning them on and off automatically at pre-set times. Use them outdoors for security lighting or indoors to make it appear that you're at home when you're away. If a fixture is controlled by two switches, purchase a three-way timer, and follow the manufacturer's wiring directions. Otherwise, buy a single-pole timer.

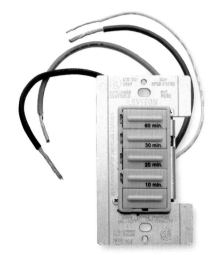

Four-Level Time-Delay Switch

A simple push of a button turns on this four-level time-delay switch for 10, 20, 30, or 60 minutes—handy for lights that you often forget to turn off. The button at the bottom acts as a simple on/off switch.

Programmable Switch

A programmable switch like this one can turn lights on and off up to six times a day and has a "random" setting intended to confuse potential burglars as to when a house is occupied. Equipped with a manual override, the timer can also function as a simple on/off switch.

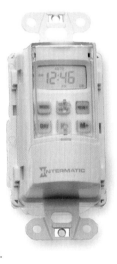

Plug-In Timer

A plug-in timer can turn a lamp or radio on and off several times a day, depending on where you position the tabs around the dial.

Time-Delay Switch

Advance the dial clockwise on this time-delay switch to turn on a fixture. Rotating the dial farther sets the timer to turn the fixture off after an interval of 1 to 60 minutes. This switch has no on/off option, so the fixture cannot be left on indefinitely.

Adding a Timer Switch

The instructions that follow apply only to timers that have a neutral (white) wire; these can be installed only in a box with two cables, as discussed on page 38. To install a timer that has no white wire, use the procedure for installing a dimmer switch, also shown on page 38.

1 Identifying the Wire that Brings Power to the Box

Shut off electricity to the circuit supplying the switch box (page 35), then take off the cover plate and remove the old switch (page 38). If you find only one black wire in the box, stop; you can't use the box for a timer that has a white wire.

Separate all the wire ends so they cannot touch each other or the box, and restore power. Carefully touch the probes of a voltage tester to each pair of black and white wires. When the tester glows, you've found the wires that bring power to the box. Turn the power off again.

2 Splicing the Ground and Neutral Wires

If there is a bare or green ground wire in the box, splice it to the switch's green ground lead (page 36). Splice the switch's white lead together with both white house wires.

3 Connecting the Hot Wires

Splice the switch's black lead to the black house wire that brings power to the box. Splice the other black house wire to the switch's remaining lead.

4 Mounting the Switch

Gently push the wires back into the box, and fasten the switch to the box with the mounting screws. Check that the switch is vertical, and adjust if necessary. Re-install the cover plate.

AN EFFICIENT LIGHT SENTRY FOR SECURITY

The procedure that follows shows how to mount a security light in place of an existing outdoor fixture, whether the new fixture has one light, as shown at right, or two. If you plan to install the light where there is no electrical box, consult Sunset's *Complete Home Wiring* for instructions on how to run cable and install a new box.

Motion sensors work poorly when aimed along a sidewalk or other approach to your house. Choose a location for the light that will permit you to aim the sensor across the most likely path of an intruder.

1 Removing the Old Fixture

Shut off power to the circuit that supplies the fixture (page 35). Working from a stable ladder, remove the mounting screws or nuts that hold the old fixture to the box, then gently pull the fixture toward you. Test to confirm that there is no power at the box.

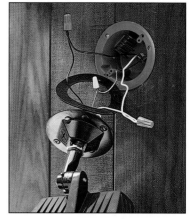

2 Connecting the Wires

Slip the security-light wires through the rubber gasket that comes with the fixture. If you detached a bare or green ground wire from the old fixture, connect it to the security light's green wire or ground screw. Splice the light's white lead to the white wire and black lead to the black wire that you detached from the old fixture.

3 Mounting the Fixture

Position the rubber gasket so it will seal moisture out of the box, and press the fixture into place. Tighten the mounting screws or nuts, and check that the seal is tight all around the fixture.

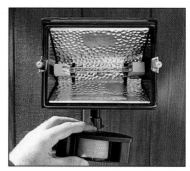

4 Aiming the Light and Sensor

Restore power to the circuit. Turn the light on during the day by flipping the house switch off and on several times. To aim the light, loosen the wing nut, point the light, and tighten the nut. Then orient the sensor as described on the facing page.

Calibrating the Sensor

1 Selecting the Field of View

Aim the sensor so it detects motion not only on the usual pathway to the house but also in your yard. The goal is that the sensor turn on the light only when someone approaches your house, and that it not respond to a car that passes on the street. Some experimenting may be necessary to point the sensor in the right direction and to adjust its sensitivity satisfactorily.

2 Setting Range and Time

Most motion detectors have two controls. On the sensor shown above, a dial adjusts sensitivity to motion. Start at the middle setting. If the light turns on as someone walks along the street far from the house, reduce the sensitivity. Increase sensitivity if someone must approach too near the house before the lights come on. A three-position switch controls how many minutes the light stays on after the sensor detects motion, 4 minutes or 12 in this case.

Motion-Sensor Options

An alternative to installing a new security light is to equip your existing fixture for security duty by adding a motion detector. If your fixture is built so that you can run a wire from a point near the light bulb socket to the surface on which the fixture is fastened, the simplest solution is a lamp-base unit (below, top.) Screw the light bulb into the unit, then screw the assembly into the fixture. Next, mount the unit's motion-sensor nearby, and adjust it as described at left.

If the design of your fixture precludes the lamp-base solution, consider having a separate motion sensor (below, bottom) wired directly to the fixture, either through a knockout hole in the canopy or by way of a new electrical box cover plate with one mounting hole for the fixture and another for the motion detector.

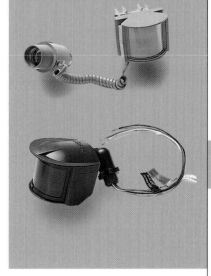

OUTDOOR LIGHTING OPTIONS

Incandescent outdoor fixtures that stay on all night consume plenty of electricity. Money-saving alternatives include not only motion-detector lights (pages 42–43) but also lights powered by the sun, low-voltage fixtures, as well as sensors and timers that turn lights off during the day. If you want a light to stay on from dusk to dawn, add a daylight sensor to the circuit. For additional control options, add a timer, or install a device that combines a daylight sensor with a timer. With such an arrangement, the sensor turns on, say, some walkway lights around sundown, and the timer can turn off the lights at an hour when they are no longer needed.

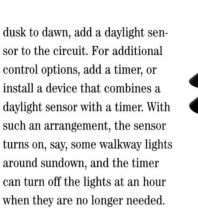

Nighttime Light from the Sun

Costing nothing to operate, solar-powered garden lights collect all the energy they need from the sun by means of solar cells mounted atop each light. These fixtures, though not exceptionally bright, can more than adequately light a pathway or accent garden foliage. Just stick them into the ground and wait. It may take a few days for the lights to achieve full brilliance.

Low-Voltage Systems

If you need illumination for a pathway, deck, or patio, consider a low-voltage lighting kit. Typically, it includes fixtures, all the cable and connectors you need, plus a transformer to lower 120-volt house current to 12 volts. Many transformers also incorporate a timer. Installation is easy. First, run the cable in shallow trenches. Then stick the lights into the ground, and link them to the cable with snap-on connectors. Mount the transformer, and plug it into a standard outdoor electrical outlet.

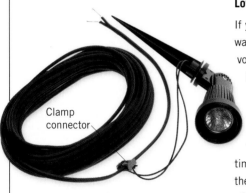

Clamp connector

Brilliant Light Outdoors

High-intensity discharge (HID) lights contain gases that enable them to radiate a lot of light using a relatively small amount of power. The most common types are mercury vapor, metal halide, and sodium. The problem with HID lights is that they are glaring and often have an unattractive green or yellow tinge. Use them only if you need very bright illumination. The mercury-vapor light shown at left is equipped with a daylight sensor.

Fluorescent Floodlights

Until recently, fluorescent tubes would not glow in cold weather, but new technology has produced tubes that operate in temperatures well below 0°F, making them suitable for outdoor applications. These lights, many of which operate at 12 volts, cost considerably less to operate than 120-volt incandescent floodlights.

Photo Cells and Timers

Daylight Sensors

Instead of buying a daylight sensor integrated with a light fixture, you can install a stand-alone sensor in an unshaded spot to control an existing outdoor light. Several such retrofits are shown at right. Most common is a large photo cell that's mounted directly onto a knockout in the outdoor fixture box. Simplest to install is a sensor that screws into the lamp base. Or opt for a discreet photo eye that's designed for installation on a lamppost.

Sensor-Timer Combo

If you have a string of plug-in outdoor lights (such as Christmas lights, Italian lights, or rope lights), attach this unit to the side of your house, and plug it into an outlet, then plug the lights into the unit. You can control the lights with its daylight sensor, its timer, or its manual on/off switch.

Heavy-Duty Outdoor Timer

There's nothing fancy about this timer; it turns lights or other electrical devices on and off once a day. But it can handle heavy loads (up to 4,100 watts), it has a rugged housing that withstands abuse, and you can lock the cover.

REMEDIES FOR KITCHEN AND LAUNDRY

Kitchen and laundry-room appliances can pick your pocket of energy dollars. But you can put a stop to the thievery with simple maintenance procedures and a few simple adjustments and repairs.

Two easily remedied shortcomings in your refrigerator can make it work harder than necessary to keep your food cold—a waste of electricity and money. One is dirty condenser coils. The solution is to clean the coils twice a year (below). The second source of wasted energy in your refrigerator is a door seal that is no longer airtight. You can solve the problem in one of the two ways shown on the next page: by realigning the door or by installing a new seal.

CLEANING CONDENSER COILS

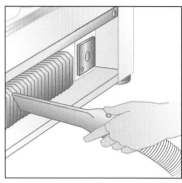

A refrigerator's condenser coils and cooling fins are located either under the unit behind a grille on the front or on the back of the appliance (left). Pull outward on the grill, unclipping it to expose the coils, or move the refrigerator away from the wall. Most refrigerators roll on wheels; however, legs at the front of the appliance used for leveling it may have lifted the wheels off the floor. If so, screw the legs upward before trying to move the refrigerator. With a long-handled brush or a vacuum cleaner hose, clean the coils, taking care not to bend the cooling fins (above). Clip the grille onto the refrigerator or push it against the wall and restore the leveling legs to their original positions.

■ SEALING IN THE COLD

The hinges of many refrigerator doors allow them to be shifted slightly to improve contact between the refrigerator case and the magnetic seal around the perimeter of the doors. On a side-by-side model, the simplest approach is to adjust the top hinge; it's easier to reach than the one at the bottom of the door.

For a refrigerator with the freezer above the refrigerator section instead of beside it, you can adjust the freezer door with the top hinge. To tackle the refrigerator door, you'll need to work with the bottom hinge.

If your refrigerator's hinges do not permit door adjustments—or if repositioning the doors doesn't solve the problem—consider replacing the old door seal with a new one (below right). You can make the job easier if you soak the new seal in a tray of warm water to make it more pliable.

ADJUSTING A REFRIGERATOR DOOR

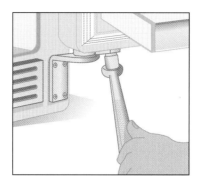

1 Loosening the Hinge
Refrigerator hinges are often concealed by snap-on covers. If you find one, lift it off the hinge. Slightly loosen the hex-head screws that secure the door. A nut driver—a tool with a screwdriver handle on one end and a wrench socket on the other—works well for the top hinge. A bottom hinge requires a socket wrench.

2 Repositioning the Door
Place a level on the top edge of the door and gently maneuver the door to make it level. Holding the door in the new position, tighten the screws and snap the hinge cover into place.

Replacing a Door Gasket

At the top of the door, curl back the old rubber gasket to reveal a metal retaining strip underneath. Loosen but do not remove the screws holding the strip in place across the top and partway down each side of the door. Remove the old gasket from this section, then slide the new gasket

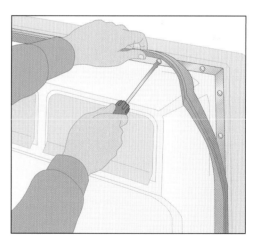

under the retaining strip and partially tighten the screws. Loosen the screws along the lower sides and bottom of the door and pull out the remainder of the old gasket. Slip the bottom half of the new gasket under the strip, then tighten all the screws.

ADJUSTING A GAS BURNER

Another energy waster in the kitchen is a gas cooktop with poorly adjusted burner flames, which increase cooking time. You can end this needless waste of energy in ten minutes with the simple fix shown at right.

1 Raising the Cooktop

Turn off all burner controls and make sure the stove's surface is cool. Remove burner grates, then raise the hinged cooktop and prop it open. Most stoves have a metal rod for this purpose under the cooktop. Find the air shutter for the burner that needs adjustment, usually located near the front of the stove, then loosen the shutter setscrew.

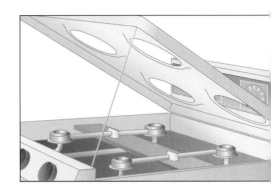

2 Fine-Tuning the Flame

Turn the burner on to its highest setting. Open the shutter slightly to turn yellow-tipped flames blue; close it to quiet a noisy, irregular flame. After adjusting the shutter, tighten the setscrew and close the cooktop.

The Perfect Flame

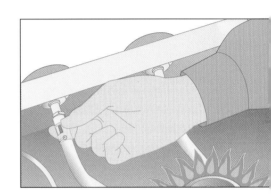

Gas burners are sensitive to the amount of air supplied to the flame. Ideally, the flame should burn steadily without flickering, and with dis-

tinct blue cones less than an inch high (above left). Too much air (above middle) causes a flame that's uneven and that often hisses or sput-

ters loudly. Too little air (above right) results in a yellow-tipped flame that can leave carbon deposits on the bottoms of cookware.

RESTORING AIRFLOW TO A CLOTHES DRYER

In the laundry room, a clean dryer is an efficient dryer. Most people know to clean the lint filter before every load, but it's equally important to delint the dryer exhaust duct every six months. A lint buildup in the duct—or at the vent where the dryer exhaust is expelled—chokes airflow through the dryer, lengthening drying times.

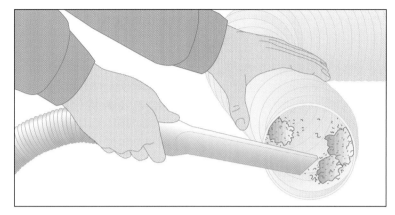

Vacuuming the Exhaust Duct

Carefully pull the dryer far enough from the wall to reach the rear panel, where the exhaust duct is attached. For a flexible duct, loosen the clamps that secure it to the dryer and to the rest of the exhaust run where it enters the wall. If the duct is metal, remove any duct tape around the joints—as well as any screws you find—and separate the pipe into sections. Tape a brush attachment to a vacuum-cleaner hose, then clean the dryer's exhaust outlet, the interior of the duct pieces you removed, and the duct in the wall as far as you can reach. Reassemble the exhaust duct as you found it. Retape joints as necessary, then move the dryer back into position.

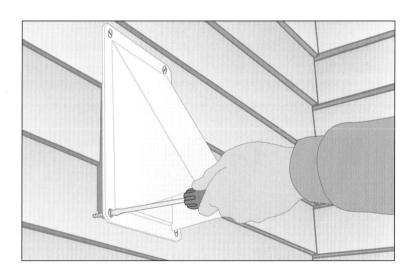

Checking the Exterior Vent

When cleaning your dryer's exhaust duct, you should also check the louvered vent where the dryer exhaust exits the house. Remove excess lint buildup with an old toothbrush. If any of the louvers is damaged, inoperative, or missing, remove the old vent and replace it with a new one available at any hardware store.

WEATHERSTRIPPING AND CAULKING

Weatherstripping and caulking are simple, cost-effective ways to keep heated or air-conditioned air where it belongs—in the house. Heating and cooling don't do much good if the air leaks right out of your home. Weatherstripping is used to seal gaps around moving parts such as doors and windows; caulking seals the gaps where nothing moves.

■ WEATHERSTRIPPING OPTIONS

There are numerous products for weatherstripping around windows and doors. They can be classified into two groups: self-stick tapes and nail-on strips. Self-stick tapes are rubber, foam, or vinyl, backed with an adhesive that is covered with a peel-off backing. These materials are a good choice for metal or vinyl windows where nailing isn't an option, especially where the parts of doors or windows press together rather than slide against one another. Self-stick tapes can easily be cut with scissors and put on in minutes.

The highest quality and longest lasting of the self-stick tapes is EPDM (ethylene-propylene-diene-monomer) rubber. EPDM retains its elasticity and insulating qualities even after years of exposure to sub-zero temperatures. Another good choice is high-density foam, which is also durable and long lasting. Closed-cell foam is waterproof, weather resistant and inexpensive but it does break down and will need to be replaced regularly. Open-cell foam can be compressed the most to seal even the narrowest of gaps, but it is only for indoor use, as it quickly degrades when exposed to the elements. Vinyl V-strips are a substitute for spring bronze; they are extremely easy to install but also wear out quickly.

Nail-on strips are the best choice for wood windows as they don't rely on adhesive and thus tend to stay in place over time. The type of nail-on strip you choose will depend on the gaps you need to seal. Gaps less than ¼ inch wide and relatively consistent in width are best sealed with spring bronze—a metal flange that is nailed in place and then "sprung" open to close the gap. This material is especially well suited for filling the gaps between a window sash and its jambs.

A vinyl tubular gasket works well where the gaps are large or inconsistent in width. This product is rubber tubing with a flange for nailing. The flange is often reinforced with metal to prevent the soft vinyl from tearing.

Felt weatherstripping is also available but it is only suitable for indoor use, since it rots quickly when it gets wet.

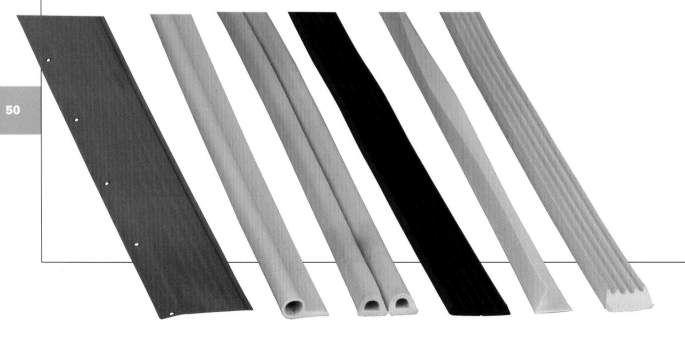

Sealing a Double-Hung Window

The most common window used in home construction, the double-hung window is also the most difficult to seal with its two sliding sashes.

Newer windows have built-in weatherstripping that creates an excellent seal; older windows often need attention, however. Installing spring bronze nail-on strips is the best way to weatherstrip wood windows. To form a complete seal, insert metal strips between the sashes and the jambs, and attach them to the top of the upper sash, the bottom of the lower sash, and to the bottom face of the upper sash.

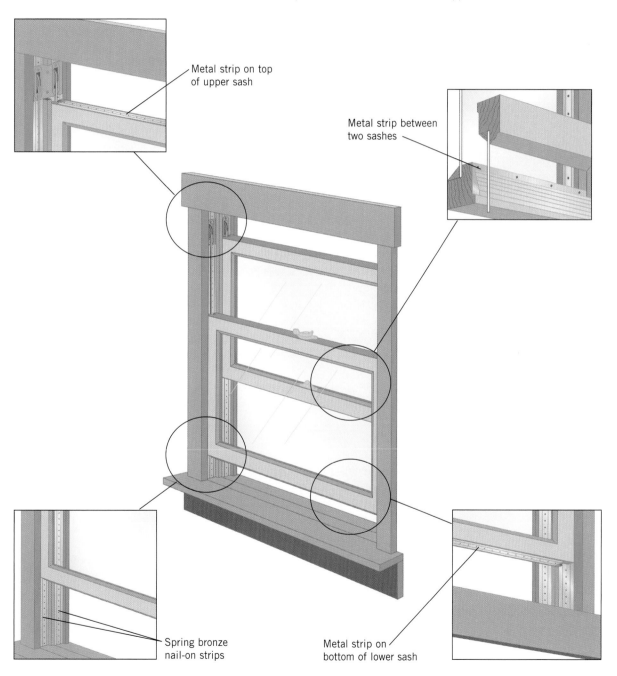

Metal strip on top of upper sash

Metal strip between two sashes

Spring bronze nail-on strips

Metal strip on bottom of lower sash

1 Prepare the Window

Before applying weatherstripping, prepare the window by scraping away loose paint or old weatherstripping. With double-hung windows, it's also a good idea to check the sash lock to make sure it's pulling the upper and lower sashes together to form a tight seal when closed. If it's not, you can correct this by repositioning one or both halves of the sash lock.

2 Attach the Vertical Strips

Measure the side channels for both sashes and cut bronze spring strips to length with a tin snips. Slide the strips up between the sash and jamb so the nailing flange butts up against the sash stop. Push the strip up until it hits the top of the window or the pulley. If your window has pulleys, cut the strip into two pieces so the bottom strip is flush with the bottom of the pulley. Then cut a shorter strip to fit above the pulley. Attach the strips to the jambs with brads. If you notice a strip is not being compressed as the sash closes, you can increase the tension on the strip by slipping a putty knife under the open end and prying gently upward. Do this a little at a time until the strip compresses without causing binding.

3 Attach the Horizontal Strips

Measure for the horizontal strips—three in all—and cut them to length so they extend the full width of the window. Attach one piece to the bottom of the lower sash so that the nailing flange is flush with the inside edge of the window. Hammer gently to prevent cracking the window. Attach the second piece to the top of the upper sash. The third piece is attached to the bottom face of the upper sash to create a seal between the sashes when the window is closed. Adjust the tension on any of these strips as you did for the vertical pieces.

Sealing the Pulleys

To prevent air leaks around the pulleys for sash cords, cover the pulleys with self-adhesive caps. Start by cleaning the pulley surface thoroughly, then peel off the backing from the cover and position it over the pulley. Pull the sash cord out to snap it into the pulley and then press the cover in place.

Pulley cover

Sash cord

Other Weatherstripping Options

There are some instances in which you can't or won't want to use spring bronze to seal a double-hung window. If the window is made of metal or vinyl, nailing isn't an option, so you'll need to use self-stick products. When gaps at the top or bottom of the window are large or uneven, self-stick foam will seal better than spring bronze. Finally, on windows where the gap between the sash and the jamb is too tight for spring bronze, tubular vinyl is an adequate substitute.

Self-Stick Foam

Self-stick foam is easy to apply. The only requirement for a good bond is a smooth, clean surface. Remove any loose paint, clean the surfaces with a mild detergent, and allow them to dry. Measure strips and cut them to length with scissors. Peel off the backing and press the foam in place.

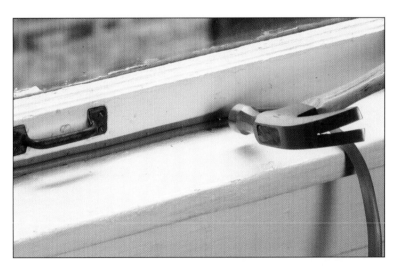

Tubular Vinyl

Unlike spring bronze and plastic V-strips, tubular gaskets are applied to the outside of the window and are thus somewhat more obvious. Here again, measure the strips and cut them to length with scissors (or tin snips if they're reinforced with metal). The secret to applying this type of weatherstripping is to butt the tube section snug up against the part to be sealed, all the while keeping tension on the strip as you drive in the brads.

Plastic Self-Adhesive V-Strips

Installation is similar to that for spring bronze (pages 51–52). Take particular care to clean the surfaces so the adhesive will stick well. Measure the pieces and cut them to length with scissors. Position as you did for spring bronze, then peel off the backing and press in place.

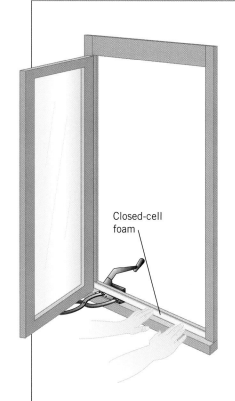

Closed-cell foam

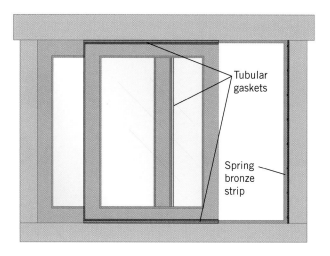

Tubular gaskets

Spring bronze strip

Sealing a Sliding Window

A sliding window is weatherstripped similarly to a double-hung one—just envision the double-hung one on its side. If only one sash moves, nail a spring bronze strip in the side channel that receives the sliding sash.

Then nail tubular gaskets along the top, bottom, and side of the sliding sash. For windows where both sashes slide, nail spring bronze strips in both side channels and attach tubular gaskets to the tops and bottoms.

Sealing a Casement Window

How you seal a casement window depends on whether it's metal, vinyl, or wood. For metal and vinyl casements, apply strips of closed-cell foam to the inside edges of the frame. Just measure, cut it to length, and press it in place. With wood frame casements, you can use nail-on spring bronze strips. On casements that open outward, attach the strips so the nailing flange is along the outside edge of the frame. This way the window will compress the strip as it closes. Reverse the position if the window swings inward.

Window Insulating Kits

An efficient, if somewhat visually intrusive, alternative to weatherstripping involves the use of replaceable window insulating kits designed to cover the windows and block drafts. When used as directed, they can increase the R-value of a single pane of glass by 90 percent.

There are two types of kits: one uses a special shrink-wrap film that is first taped to the inside window frames and then heated with a hair dryer or heat gun to eliminate wrinkles. These materials are not strong enough to stand up to use outdoors.

The other kit type uses a heavier plastic sheathing that is either tacked or stapled to the window exteriors with cardboard strips to reinforce the fastened edges.

Weatherstrip Your Doors

Because doors have fewer moving parts than windows, they're generally easier to seal, presuming they are in something close to their proper alignment. To add weatherstripping so it doesn't cause binding, it's best to even out the gaps around the door before starting work. Reset and shim hinges as needed to create uniform gaps.

The weatherstripping you'll use to seal a door is the same as that used for a window. Spring bronze or plastic V-strips do a good job for the top and sides. The bottom, however, presents a different challenge, especially where foot traffic is heavy. Standard weatherstripping, even metal strips, would wear out quickly under heavy use. There are a number of special seals designed for door bottoms, including door sweeps, door shoes, and thresholds.

A door sweep attaches to the bottom face of the door; its rubber gasket drags along the floor or threshold to create a seal. A door shoe fits on the bottom edge of the door with a flexible gasket pressing tightly against the floor or threshold. A metal threshold with a rubber gasket, on the other hand, presses against the bottom

of the door to stop drafts. These components can be used independently or in combination when necessary. For example, when the gap below a door is too large to be spanned by a single gasket, a door shoe and a threshold can be combined to create a seal. Garage doors have their own special seals, typically rubber gaskets that attach to the bottom of the door and to the side and top jambs.

A gap as small as ¼ inch along the bottom of a 36-inch-wide door is the equivalent of having a 3-inch-square hole in the door. Fortunately, there are straightforward solutions to sealing such gaps.

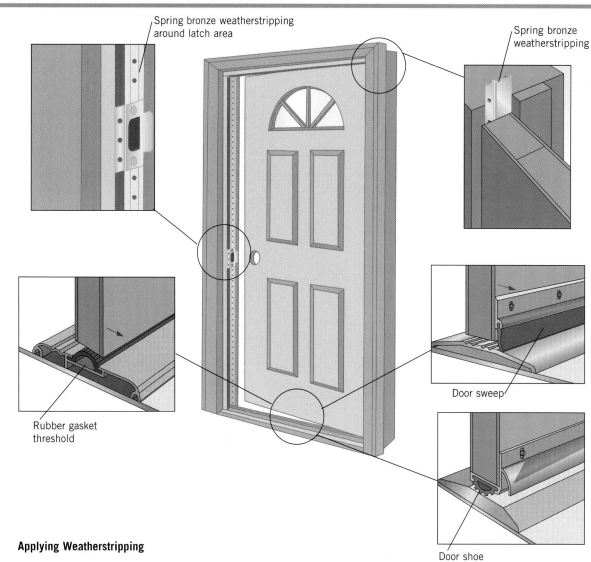

Spring bronze weatherstripping around latch area

Spring bronze weatherstripping

Rubber gasket threshold

Door sweep

Door shoe

Applying Weatherstripping

To weatherstrip a door, begin by cutting a short strip of spring bronze for the latch area. This piece fits behind the strike plate up against the door stop. In most cases you'll need to bend or trim this piece so that it doesn't interfere with the strike plate or latch mechanism. Attach the strip with brads, and then measure and cut strips for the rest of the latch side, then the top and the opposite side. If you're working with plastic V-strip, you can often apply the latch strip to the stop as plastic V-strips are narrower than spring bronze.

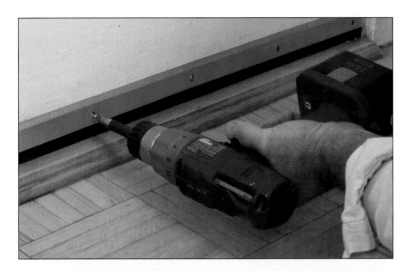

Installing a Door Sweep

A door sweep is the simplest seal to apply to a door bottom because you can leave the door on its hinges. Just measure the width of the door and cut the sweep to match. Then screw it to the base of the door positioned so that it contacts the threshold while still allowing the door to swing freely open and shut.

Installing a Threshold

To replace an old wood threshold, start by cutting it in two, taking care to protect the adjacent flooring. Pry up the pieces and save them to help you mark the length on the new threshold. Place the pieces on the new metal frame and allow for the thickness of the blade you used to cut them. Mark the new piece at that length. Then cut the new threshold to length with a tin snips or hacksaw. Test the fit and when it is snug, remove it and apply two beads of silicone to the flooring. Reposition the threshold and attach it with the screws provided. Finally, trim the gasket to length if needed and fit it into the threshold. Rubber gasket thresholds eventually wear out with heavy use. But once you have the metal frame in place, replacing a worn gasket is a 5-minute job.

Installing a Door Shoe

Door shoes require a little more work, but create a better seal because the "fingers" on the bottom compress tightly against the threshold. You will more than likely need to trim the door to allow for the thickness of the shoe. If you have any doubts about your ability to trim the door precisely, hire a carpenter; mistakes can be costly. To determine how much you'll need to trim, open the door and slip the shoe into place. Then measure from the bottom of the shoe to the bottom of the door. Remove the shoe, close the door, and transfer this measurement onto the door near each corner, measuring from the top of the threshold. Take the door off its hinges and lay it across sawhorses, then draw a line to connect the marks. Clamp a straightedge to the door to guide a circular saw in cutting along the line. Remove any splinters with sandpaper, slip on the shoe, and attach it with screws. Hang the door and check to make sure it seals without binding.

SEAL NON-MOVING PARTS WITH CAULK

Often referred to as sealant, caulk comes in cartridges for use in a caulk gun or in smaller tubes that are squeezed by hand. The best caulk to use to seal air leaks is silicone, as it stays flexible for a long time (50 years according to some manufacturer's guarantees). Silicone cannot be painted, however. If you must paint, use an acrylic latex caulk with silicone.

■ IDENTIFYING AND LOCATING AIR LEAKS

In order to stop the unwanted air flow through your home, you need to identify what is driving the air. Anyone who has felt a chilly draft on a windy day has detected a wind-effect leak—air forced through the house by wind.

Wind Effect

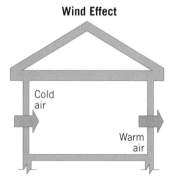

Less obvious are the stack-effect leaks. These often combine to create larger energy losses than those due to the wind. Stack-effect leaks are caused by warm air rising through the house in much the same way as hot air rises through

Stack Effect

a chimney. The difference is that, in winter, you're paying to heat this air. The lost heated air sometimes travels in convoluted paths—through cracks in the foundation, up through interior walls, through penetrations in ceilings. However it gets there, it exits the house. Odds are, you've got both wind-effect and stack-effect leaks in your house.

Wind-effect leaks are easy to find. On a windy day, hold a coat hanger with tissue or kitchen plastic draped over it near your doors and windows. Fluttering indicates a wind effect leak and will most

likely need to be treated by the addition of weatherstripping (see pages 50–54).

Stack-effect leaks are tougher to find; you'll need to do a bit of detective work. The two main areas in which to concentrate your search are the foundation and the attic. Start by inspecting the foundation from the inside. Look for cracks in concrete or gaps in cinder blocks, paying particular attention to the mortar between blocks. Mark any defects for later caulking or fill them on the spot. Also check for gaps between the foundation and the framing that rests upon it. Poorly fitting basement windows are another common source of problems.

In the attic, inspect plumbing vent stacks and chimneys passing through to the roof. Attic access panels or doors are also problem areas. Look for open floor joist ends in kneewall attics and keep an eye out for dirty insulation. This can be a telltale sign of a leak. The fiberglass insulation filters out the dirt as air passes through it. And if it's not trapping air, it's not insulating for you.

In the interior of the house, look for gaps between drywall and trim, around electrical and plumbing openings, and where recessed lights and hood fans penetrate the ceilings or walls.

Seal Doors and Windows

Even if windows and doors are sealed with weatherstripping, they can still allow a copious flow of air through gaps between the rough opening and the window or door jambs. The best way to seal these gaps is to remove the interior trim and fill up the space with *non-expanding* foam. Remove the trim carefully by prying it up with a wide-blade putty knife and a pry bar. Trim off excess foam with a utility knife and re-install the trim. A simpler but, also more visible, alternative is to leave the interior trim in place and seal around it with a clear silicone caulk or paintable latex caulk with silicone.

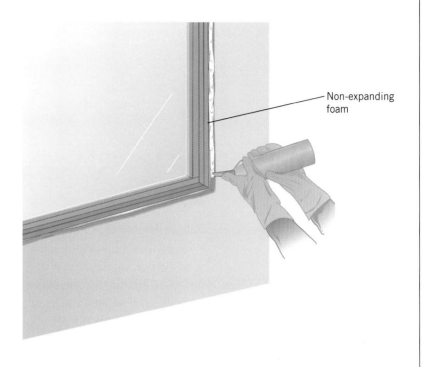

Non-expanding foam

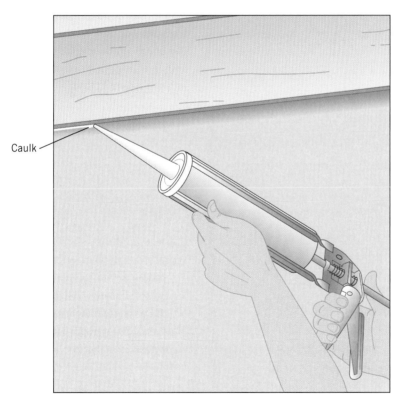

Caulk

Seal Around the Foundation

The basement or foundation is where most cold air enters the home. Air can slip in behind siding where it overlaps the foundation. Prevent this by forcing caulk up under the siding. Also fill any cracks or gaps in the foundation with silicone caulk, and apply caulk at the junction of dissimilar materials, such as where metal flashing meets wood or concrete.

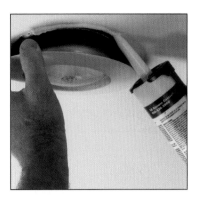

Seal Electrical Switches and Receptacles

Even if you seal the penetrations around electrical conduits and cables as they pass through ceilings and floors, air may find a way to get to the switches and receptacles. You can seal the space around the electrical box by removing the cover plate and installing an insulator. Alternatively, remove the cover plate and fill the gaps with non-expanding foam. Stop air from passing through the receptacle itself by plugging unused slots with insulated covers.

Seal the Baseboards

Inside the house, air can easily slip through gaps at the bottom edges of the drywall. The most effective way to stop this is to remove the baseboards and fill the gaps with non-expanding insulating foam.

Check Recessed Lighting and Drop Ceilings

As air rises on its way toward the attic, it often finds a path through recessed lighting fixtures. Remove the trim pieces and seal around the edges with caulk. Better yet, replace the lights with UL-approved airtight fixtures. Drop ceilings are another common path, since they hide cracks, gaps, and penetrations in the original ceiling. Remove the ceiling tiles and fill cracks and gaps with caulk. Seal around any penetrations with non-expanding foam.

Seal Plumbing, Heating, and Electrical Penetrations

Air moving up through a house often follows the plumbing or electrical lines and slips through the penetrations where they pass through the walls, cabinets, and floors. The best way to close off these exits is to follow the lines yourself and seal around the penetrations with non-expanding insulating foam. For plumbing, follow both the supply and the waste lines. Check in cabinets, under floors, and in the attic. Seal around exterior vents from bathrooms or kitchen exhaust fans with silicone caulk.

Seal Attic Bypasses or Chases

Another way that air travels up into attics is through bypasses or chases. These are framed shafts for electrical or plumbing lines that run from a basement or ground floor up into an attic. Vent stacks for plumbing often run through a chase, and the openings at the top and bottom may need to be filled with expanding foam or plastic bags filled with fiberglass insulation. Chimneys are also sometimes enclosed in this way. Any gaps around the chimney as it passes into the attic should be filled with a non-combustible insulation such as rockwool.

Seal Attic Knee Spaces

Attics that have been converted to living spaces typically have short walls, called knee walls, between the floor and the roof. The area behind knee walls is often used for storage and it's important to weatherstrip and insulate any access doors into this space. Enclosures should also be built around built-ins, such as drawers, so that they can be insulated and sealed. Air can also leak from interior walls downstairs, entering the attic through its floor joists. You can block this air flow with plastic bags filled with fiberglass insulation, forced into the open joist spaces.

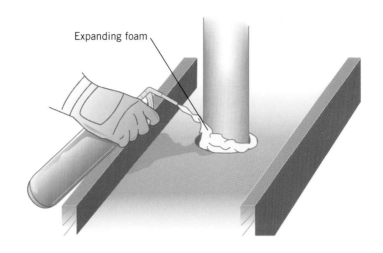

Expanding foam

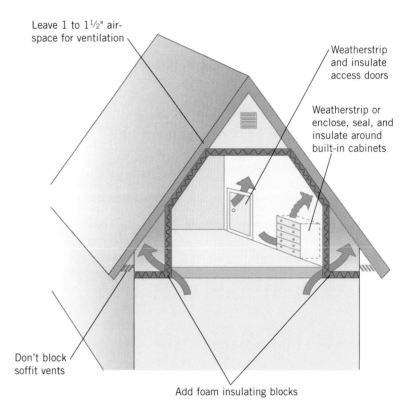

Leave 1 to 1½" air-space for ventilation

Weatherstrip and insulate access doors

Weatherstrip or enclose, seal, and insulate around built-in cabinets

Don't block soffit vents

Add foam insulating blocks

INSTALLING A PROGRAMMABLE THERMOSTAT

Replacing an old, single-setting thermostat with a programmable model (at right) is one of the quickest and easiest ways to save energy dollars. These instruments improve on the automatic temperature control of ordinary thermostats by allowing you to prescribe different temperatures for different times of the day or week. A typical programmable thermostat has one programming cycle for weekdays and another for the weekend. For each cycle, the thermostat lets you set four times and temperatures, corresponding to waking, leaving the house, returning, and sleeping.

When buying a thermostat, look for one with a manual override and a hold-temperature button. These features enable the thermostat to maintain a tempera-ture not specified in any of the cycles—handy for vacations and other long absences. A push of a button restores the thermostat to normal, programmed operation.

Programmable thermostats, like non-programmable models, are designed to work with most heating and air-conditioning systems having 2, 3, 4, or 5 wires connected to the thermostat. If your house has electric baseboard heating, do not attempt to install this kind of thermostat. It won't work with the high voltage required by baseboard heating.

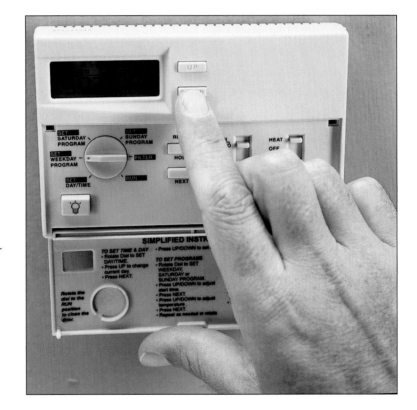

1 Detaching the Wires

Turn off the power to the furnace at the breaker panel or fuse box (page 35). Check the snap-on cover of the old thermostat for retaining screws and remove any that you find. Pull off the cover, and disconnect one wire at a time from the thermostat, labeling each wire with the letter next to its terminal. Bend the wires so they don't slip through the hole in the thermostat base.

2 Removing the Thermostat

Loosen the thermostat mounting screws, then pull the thermostat and wiring away from the wall, grabbing the wires where they emerge from the wall. Set the old thermostat aside without letting go of the wires. Wrap them around a pencil—or use a clothespin or binder clip—to prevent them from disappearing into the hole in the wall. If necessary, strip each wire to bare at least $\frac{1}{2}$ inch of copper, then clean the metal with steel wool or emery cloth.

3 Mounting the New Thermostat

Separate the body of the new thermostat from the base. Remove the pencil holding the wires, then thread them through the base and below the terminal block. Resecure the wires with the pencil. Pack paper towels into the hole in the wall to protect the thermostat from drafts. Hold the base against the wall with a torpedo level resting on top and mark the wall for mounting holes. In wood, drill holes for screws; in drywall, drill holes for plastic screw anchors (supplied with most thermostats). Screw the base to the wall.

4 Finishing the Job

Consult the manufacturer's instructions to determine which wire goes to which terminal on the new thermostat. As you connect the wires, keep them from touching each other or other parts of the thermostat. When the wiring is complete, install the back-up batteries to prevent the thermostat from losing its program in a power failure, and attach the body. Restore power to the heating and cooling system and program the thermostat according to your wishes and the manufacturer's instructions.

GET THE AIR MOVING

The idea of letting hot summer air into your home to help keep it cool sounds paradoxical. But some parts of your house need to be well ventilated both summer and winter, regardless of the temperature outdoors. In temperate weather, a whole-house fan that pulls cool, outside air through the entire house can substantially reduce the money you spend on air conditioning.

Ceiling fans circulating air within a room also help cut cooling bills. They do so by gently drawing cool air up from the floor, where it tends to collect on hot days. Reversed in winter, a ceiling fan circulates warm air that accumulates near the ceiling.

■ HELPING YOUR HOUSE BREATHE

When the weather sizzles, ventilation keeps attic spaces from overheating and radiating heat into living spaces below (right, top). The heat flowing from the attic causes your air conditioner to work harder at greater expense to you. Even attic floors that are well insulated can't withstand the onslaught of all this heat. What will help is a series of vents that allow the warm air normally trapped inside to flow up and out of the roof, to be replaced by cooler air brought into the attic by

way of the eaves. Results can be dramatic. Ventilating an attic can easily lower the temperature from 150° F to 115° F.

In winter (right, center), ventilation clears the attic of warm, moist air that may seep upward from living spaces below. Allowed to remain in the cooler attic, this humid air would deposit its moisture as condensation, not only on joists and rafters, but also in attic insulation, reducing its effectiveness.

Cold air directly below the roof also helps avert ice dams—the buildup of ice along eaves that can cause roof leaks. Keeping the roof at a uniformly cold temperature prevents snow on the upper, often warmer parts of a roof from melting, then refreezing at the eaves.

During summer months, a whole-house fan can draw in cool air through open doors and windows and exhaust it through the attic (right, bottom). Be sure to turn off the fan when you close the windows and doors. If you don't, the fan motor, straining to pull air through closed windows, will quickly burn out.

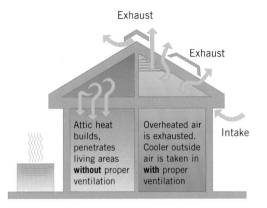

Exhaust

Exhaust

Intake

Attic heat builds, penetrates living areas **without** proper ventilation

Overheated air is exhausted. Cooler outside air is taken in **with** proper ventilation

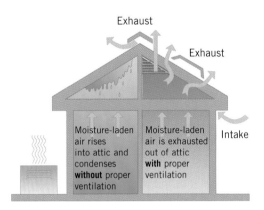

Exhaust

Exhaust

Intake

Moisture-laden air rises into attic and condenses **without** proper ventilation

Moisture-laden air is exhausted out of attic **with** proper ventilation

■ A WORLD OF VENTS

House vents come in a wide variety of shapes, sizes, and types. Intake vents are designed to fit in soffits or under eaves. Soffit vents (below) are metal louvers that run

the entire length of the soffits uninterrupted. They're most often used in new construction or when eaves or soffits are replaced.

Eave vents are often circular in shape. They are set into the eaves, one to each space between rafters, on two sides of the house, and are usually used for adding ventilation to an existing attic. To be effective, both soffit and eave vents must not be blocked by attic insulation. Rafter vents (page 75) are often used to keep insulation installed between rafters from impeding airflow from the soffit to exhaust vents high on the roof.

Exhaust vents remove moisture-laden air in both summer and winter. For maximum effect, they should be placed as close as possible to the peak of the roof. Only the ridge vent sits at the highest point of the roof. The ridge vent is

a metal extrusion that covers a gap built or cut into the roof sheathing at the ridge. Louvers in the vent allow air to escape while preventing rain from entering. Ridge vents run the full length of the roof and can be installed in any ridge, not only during construction or reroofing, but as a stand-alone project as well.

Next behind ridge vents in effectiveness are roof vents (above). These are typically small, square metal structures also built to let air pass but keep rain out. Some are equipped with a thermostatically controlled fan to speed the removal of hot air from the attic. Turbine vents (below) have specially shaped vanes that turn in the slightest breeze to pull hot and humid air out of the attic.

Gable vents (above) are very common on older homes and can be either rectangular in shape or triangular to fit into the angled space at the roof's peak. Because they're located at the ends of the attic, they're not as effective as the other vents, which either extend the length of the attic or are spaced evenly along its length. However, gable vents are the easiest to install.

Foundation vents (above) help prevent moisture from building up under homes by providing continuous airflow through crawl spaces.

■ INSTALLING A CEILING FAN

Ceiling fans, which can help warm you in winter as well as cool you in summer, are easy to install. Many have optional lighting kits, permitting you to substitute a fan and light assembly for an overhead light fixture. A ceiling fan requires 7 feet of clearance between the fan blades and the floor. For a room smaller than 225 square feet, buy a 42-inch or 44-inch fan. Larger spaces require a 52-inch fan.

Most people replacing a light fixture with a fan-and-light assembly wire the installation so that the switch controls the light (below, left). That's fine if you can reach the fan's pull switch to turn it on or if you don't object to a chain descending into the room. Alternatively, you can install a second switch, wired as shown below right, or you can buy a fan with a remote control.

One person can install a ceiling fan. However, the motor weighs about 40 pounds, so a helper might come in handy for some parts of the installation. Before beginning work, turn off power to the fan circuit at the service panel (page 35).

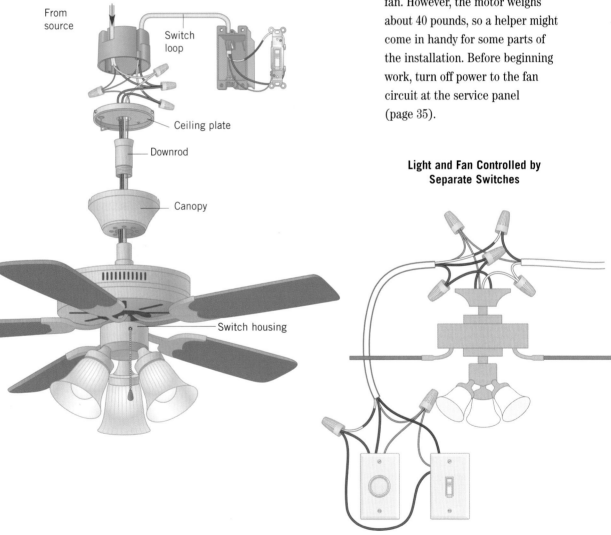

Light Controlled by Switch, Fan Controlled by Pull Chain

From source

Switch loop

Ceiling plate

Downrod

Canopy

Switch housing

Light and Fan Controlled by Separate Switches

1 Reinforcing a Ceiling Box

Take down the light fixture that the fan is to replace (page 36), and examine the ceiling box. If it is bolted through the center to a bar hanger between two joists, proceed to Step 2. If not, buy a heavy-duty bar hanger like the one shown above. Remove the ceiling box, then insert the bar hanger through the hole in the ceiling, resting its feet on the drywall. Turn the center of the bar to jam the feet against the joists on either side of the hole, then tighten the bar hanger with an adjustable wrench to force the teeth on each end into the joists. Fasten the box to the bar hanger using the U-bolt and nuts that come with it.

2 Connecting the Downrod

Push the fan's downrod (facing page) through the canopy from behind, and feed the wires from the fan motor through the downrod and canopy (above). Join the downrod to the motor, and tighten the screws that hold the two pieces together.

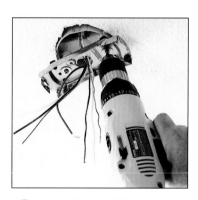

3 Attaching the Ceiling Plate

Feed the wires from the electrical box through the fan ceiling plate and fasten it to the box with screws. Then hang the fan temporarily from the hook built into the ceiling plate for this purpose. (If your ceiling plate has no hook, improvise one from a wire coat hanger.)

4 Wiring the Fan

Consult the manufacturer's wiring directions, which vary according to the number of switches controlling the fan. Make the connections with wire nuts (above), then press the wires into the electrical box. Unhook the fan and slip the canopy over the ceiling plate. Secure the canopy with the screws provided, and attach the fan blades.

5 Connecting a Light

If your fan has a light fixture, connect its wires to the fan's lighting wires in the switch housing, usually black to black and white to white (above). Fasten the fixture to the fan with the screws supplied, and add light bulbs.

INSULATION ESSENTIALS

Heat passes through ceilings, walls, and floors from the warm side to the cool side. Insulation slows this transfer of heat out of a heated house in winter and into a cooled one in summer. A well-insulated house requires less heating and cooling to maintain a comfortable indoor climate, and that translates directly into smaller energy bills.

How much insulation you need depends on where you live and the part of the house to be insulated. But the kind of insulation and how much of it you already have also figure in the calculation. In an unfinished space, you can easily measure insulation thickness. The photographs on the facing page can help you identify the type of insulation that you have.

To check finished exterior walls for insulation, remove an outlet coverplate near the baseboard. Reach into the wall beside the box with a coat-hanger wire bent into a hook and fish out some insulation. Between a floor and a ceiling, drill a ⅜-inch hole through the floor in an inconspicuous space. Gently stand a soda straw in the hole and mark it at floor level. Subtract the distance from the mark to the end of the straw from the height of your joists plus flooring to gauge how thick the insulation is.

The illustration below shows both where to check for insulation and where to add some if you find none or not enough. A climate map and companion chart on page 70 show how much insulation you need, depending on where you live. Instructions begin on page 71 for insulating just about every part of your house—including your water heater and hot water pipes.

Where to Insulate

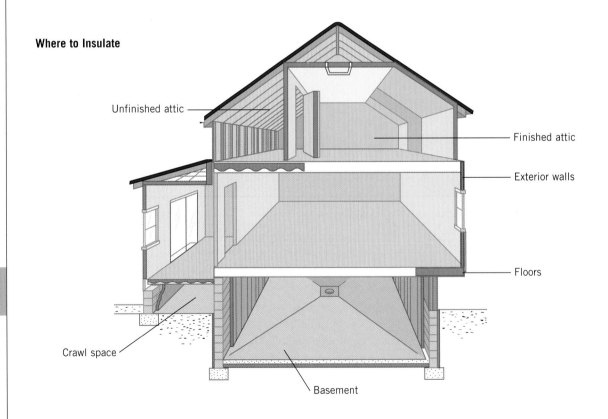

Unfinished attic

Finished attic

Exterior walls

Floors

Crawl space

Basement

Types of Insulation

	Description	**Where to Use**	**Installation Method**
Batts and Blankets 	Flexible rolls (blankets) or precut strips (batts) of fiberglass. Batts are easiest to handle, but blankets can be cut for a perfect fit.	Unfinished walls, attic floors, and floors over unheated basements and crawl spaces. Good choice with standard stud and joist spacing in uncovered surfaces.	Precut to fit between studs and joists, and can be used both between and on top of attic floor joists.
Loose Fill 	Loose fibers or granules of cellulose, fiberglass, rock wool, and other materials.	Usually blown into wall and ceiling cavities with special blowing machines. The loose material easily fills nooks and crannies.	Good choice for finished walls, unfinished attics, and hard-to-reach locations.
Rigid Foam 	Made from extruded or expanded plastic foam that has been formed into panels. Expensive but offers higher R-values per inch than other products.	Basement walls (interior and exterior), concrete floors, and some roof applications.	Usually glued in place and covered with a finish material, such as flooring or drywall.

HOW MUCH DO YOU NEED?

Developed by the United States Department of Energy, the map and chart below show how much insulation your house needs, depending on its location and the fuel you use for heating. Amounts of insulation are given as R-values—the higher the R-value, the thicker the insulation. Before insulating, also check your local building code. It may suggest somewhat higher or lower R-values.

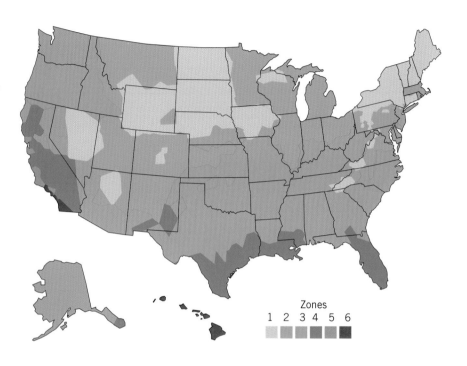

Zones
1 2 3 4 5 6

Zone	Gas	Heat Pump	Fuel Oil	Electric Furnace	Attic	Wall	Floor	Crawl Space	Basement
1	X	X	X		R-49	R-18	R-25	R-19	R-11
1				X	R-49	R-28	R-25	R-19	R-19
2	X	X	X		R-49	R-18	R-25	R-19	R-11
2				X	R-49	R-22	R-25	R-19	R-19
3	X	X	X	X	R-49	R-18	R-25	R-19	R-11
4	X	X	X		R-38	R-13	R-13	R-19	R-11
4				X	R-49	R-18	R-25	R-19	R-11
5	X				R-38	R-13	R-11	R-13	R-11
5		X	X		R-38	R-13	R-13	R-19	R-11
5				X	R-49	R-18	R-25	R-19	R-11
6	X				R-22	R-11	R-11	R-11	R-11
6		X	X		R-38	R-13	R-11	R-13	R-11
6				X	R-49	R-18	R-25	R-19	R-11

INSULATING AN UNFINISHED ATTIC

Insulating your attic is often the most important insulation project that you can undertake. First, determine the R-value of any insulation you already have (right, top). To find out how much insulation to add, subtract your finding from the R-value recommended on the facing page. You may put new insulation over old, and you need not match types. Before beginning, isolate any light fixtures between joists as shown on page 72.

When working in an unfinished attic, step only on joists, never between them. Better yet, place 1 by 6s, 1 by 8s, or strips of ¾-inch plywood next to each other atop three or four adjacent joists to serve as a work platform.

Controlling Moisture

Water vapor that condenses inside insulation ruins it. The solution is to install a vapor barrier. Some kinds of rigid foam insulation serve as their own vapor barrier. Polyethylene sheeting works well with most insulation. Fiberglass batts and blankets are available with a vapor-retardant facing on one side. Vapor barriers are most often placed on the interior side of the insulation, but in hot, humid climates, they go on the exterior side.

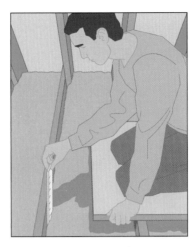

Vapor-retardant facing down

Measuring Attic Insulation

Kneeling safely on plywood, slip a ruler between the joist and insulation to measure its thickness. Average several measurements taken from different parts of the attic, then multiply the average by the R-value per inch of insulation (see table).

Fiberglass (batts/blankets)	R-3.0/in.
Fiberglass (loose fill)	R-2.5/in.
Cellulose (loose fill)	R-3.4/in.
Rock wool (loose fill)	R-2.8/in.

Installing Batts and Blankets

If the attic floor is uninsulated, use insulation with a vapor-retardant face and place the facing next to the ceiling. In hot, humid climates—or if the attic is already insulated—use unfaced fiberglass. Start at the perimeter and work toward the attic access door. Place the insulation between joists, cutting it to length as shown on page 75. For higher R-values, lay additional insulation across the joists.

Adding Loose-Fill Insulation

Rent or borrow a loose-fill insulation blower from a home center, making sure you have enough hose to reach all corners of your attic. With a helper to load the blower with insulation as needed, start at the perimeter of the attic and work toward the attic access door. Fill every joist space completely and evenly with the insulation, leaving attic vents uncovered. Level uneven spots with a rake.

KEEPING INSULATION AWAY FROM RECESSED LIGHTS

Insulation added too close to sources of intense heat can pose a fire hazard. Many attics contain recessed light fixtures that illuminate rooms below. In doing so, they can reach temperatures exceeding the ignition point of common insulation materials. Unless a fixture is rated "IC," for insulation contact, build a barrier around it to keep the insulation at least 3 inches away.

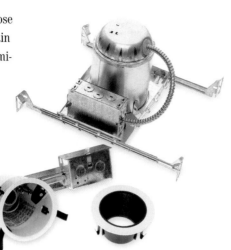

Insulation Safety
Direct contact with insulation, especially fiberglass, can cause skin irritation. Dress for safety by wearing a long-sleeved shirt, gloves, goggles, and a dust mask. Do not install insulation near flames, such as a water heater pilot light, nor around bare stovepipes, electrical fixtures, or other heat-producing equipment. Always follow the manufacturer's directions.

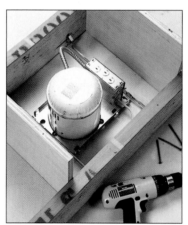

When using batts or blankets to cover the attic floor no higher than the top of the joists, create an insulation barrier by nailing two blocks of wood between joists. You can cut the blocks from a 1x or a 2x board. Nail through the joists into the ends of the blocks.

If you plan to blow insulation into the attic—or to install batts or blankets thicker than the height of the joists—build a tall plywood box around the fixture. Cut the sides at least twice as high as the joists, then nail them to the joists. Finish the box by nailing or gluing the ends to the sides. Tape newspaper over the box temporarily when blowing in loose-fill insulation to keep it from settling around the light fixture.

INSULATION FOR A STUD WALL

For walls whose studs are exposed—not uncommon in garages, for example—fiberglass batts are usually the best insulation choice, although blankets will also work. Walls are usually framed with studs spaced 16 inches or 24 inches on center, and fiberglass batts are available to fit snugly into either of these spaces. If you use unfaced insulation as in the left and center photographs below, you'll need to staple a layer of vapor-retardant polyethylene plastic over the insulation to keep it dry. Batts and blankets with a vapor-retardant facing (below, right) save this step.

Cutting Fiberglass Insulation

Place the fiberglass batt on a piece of plywood as a cutting board. Measure the height of the space between studs you wish to insulate and transfer it to the batt, laying a 2 by 4 or other straightedge across the batt to serve as a cutting guide. Compress the insulation with the cutting guide, then slice through the fiberglass with multiple strokes of a sharp utility knife.

Working Around Obstructions

To fit insulation behind wires or pipes that pass through studs, peel the front half of the batt away from the back half (above). Slide one half of the batt behind the obstruction, then cover it with the other. Around electrical boxes for receptacles and light switches, split the batt unequally, so that the thinner part fits behind the box. Cut out the front section with scissors or a utility knife for a snug fit around the box.

Attaching Faced Batts

Fiberglass batts and blankets with vapor-retardant facing on one side have flaps along the edges. Tuck the insulation between studs with the facing visible to you as you work (above), then staple the flaps to the studs.

BLOWING INSULATION INTO A WALL

If the exterior walls of your house need insulation, you can add it to the spaces between studs without removing drywall or paneling. The best choice is often blown-in cellulose, which flows past obstructions in the wall and fills cavities around existing insulation better than other loose-fill products. Furthermore, it seals air leaks, making a separate vapor barrier unnecessary.

Although many homeowners prefer to leave the job of insulating finished walls to a professional contractor, others have achieved satisfactory results for themselves. The idea is to blow insulation into each space between studs, one at a time. Doing so requires that you cut a 2- to 3-inch hole in the

wall between each pair of studs and as near the top of the stud space as possible. A hole saw in an electric drill makes short work of this part of the job. Save the drywall cutouts for repairing the holes later.

Feed the blower hose deeply into each cavity while a helper operates the blower and controls the mix of air and cellulose. Plugging the hole around the hose with a rag prevents insulation from escaping. As the space fills, gradually withdraw the hose from the hole.

KEEPING HEAT IN A CONVERTED GARAGE

A garage converted to living space needs the same level of insulation in the ceiling, walls, and floor as the main part of your house. To supplement insulation already installed in the garage, you can blow cellulose into walls (above). Insulate the floor with rigid foam boards, as you would a basement floor (page 78). If the garage is under the house, you need not insulate the ceiling. However, an above-ground garage needs the same level of ceiling insulation as the top floor of your house. Like adding insulation to the ceiling of a finished attic, this job may well require the services of a pro.

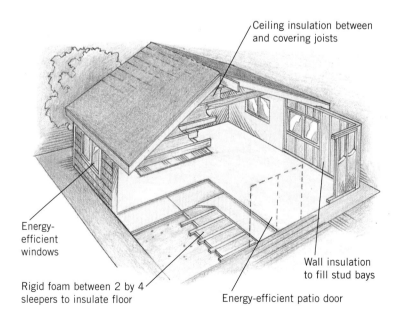

Ceiling insulation between and covering joists

Energy-efficient windows

Rigid foam between 2 by 4 sleepers to insulate floor

Wall insulation to fill stud bays

Energy-efficient patio door

Adding Insulation to a Finished Attic

Uninsulated space in a finished attic is an oven in summer, a refrigerator in winter. So, in all likelihood, your attic living space already has some insulation. If not—or if what's there is insufficient—you can add more.

Insulating this space before the drywall is fastened to the ceiling and knee walls—short walls near the eaves—is no more difficult than insulating exposed studs, joists, or rafters elsewhere in the house. However, once wall and ceiling coverings are in place, the task becomes much more complicated and can require tearing down the ceiling and walls. Unless you are an adventurous and accomplished carpenter, call in a professional.

Two Approaches

In a finished attic, insulation is installed above the ceiling in all cases. Below the ceiling, the insulation can follow the knee walls to the attic floor, then across toward the eaves (above, top). Or if your house has storage space behind the knee walls, the insulation follows the rafters to the eaves (above, bottom). In both arrangements, the insulation is installed with the vapor barrier toward the interior of the house.

Maintaining Ventilation

If your roof is equipped with soffit and ridge vents, have your insulation contractor check for ventilation between the insulation and the roof.

To assure adequate ventilation, install rafter vents (below) between rafters. Stapled to the roof decking, the vents allow a continuous airflow from the soffit to the ridge even after insulation batts have been placed over them. The vents also keep moisture from the roof from soaking the insulation. With the rafter vents in place, the spaces between rafters can be filled. For maximum R-value, cover the batts with rigid foam insulation, then finish with drywall.

Continuous layer of insulation

Insulation run along the rafters

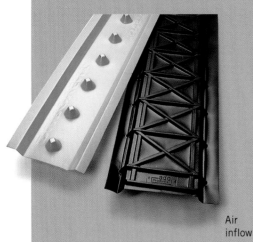

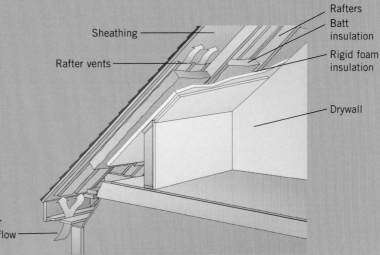

Sheathing

Rafter vents

Air inflow

Rafters

Batt insulation

Rigid foam insulation

Drywall

INSULATING BASEMENT WALLS

The walls of a basement can be insulated in several different ways. Two of the most common techniques—building a 2 by 4 stud wall for batts or blankets and gluing rigid foam boards to the wall—are shown on these pages. Either method requires that you also insulate the rim joist (below).

Insulating the Rim Joist

When insulating a basement wall, tuck insulation along the rim (or band) joist, which you'll find atop the foundation. Cut pieces of fiberglass or rigid foam insulation to fit snugly between the foundation and the sub-flooring above.

■ INSULATING BETWEEN STUDS

Besides providing cavities for batts or blankets, building a stud wall makes it possible to hide pipes and electrical wiring and offers a solid backing for drywall should you later decide to finish the basement.

Most construction specialists agree that a basement stud wall needs a vapor retardant, usually a layer of 6-mil polyethylene. But there is some dispute about where to put it—against the basement wall or on the interior of the stud wall (right).

Often the best choice depends on your climate, soil conditions, and the construction of your foundation. If your local building code doesn't decide the matter for you, ask a builder or knowledgeable folks at your building supply store about local practice.

Do not, however, install a vapor barrier in both locations. Doing so can trap moisture within.

To frame a wall, lay a sole (bottom) plate of pressure-treated 2 by 4s end to end on the floor. Position the sole plate an inch or two from the wall. Directly above the sole plate, nail a top plate to floor joists, then nail studs to both plates. Space the studs 24 inches apart—or closer together to build, say, a frame around a window.

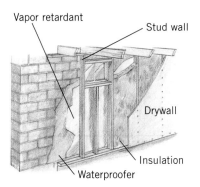

Vapor Barrier Against the Basement Wall

This basement wall has been coated with a masonry waterproofer, then lined with a vapor barrier of over-lapping polyethylene sheets taped to each other and to the wall. Use this method if, despite your best efforts, moisture continues to find its way through your basement walls. Any dampness that penetrates the wall will stop at the vapor barrier.

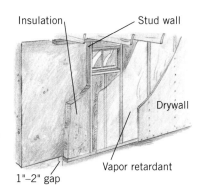

Vapor Barrier Inside the Stud Wall

This option treats the basement wall just like walls in the upper floors of the house, where the vapor barrier is placed on the warm side, normally the interior of the framed wall. This approach is usually best if your foundation is waterproof and well drained, as are many foundations made of solid concrete.

■ INSTALLING RIGID FOAM BOARDS

An alternative to stud walls for insulating a basement (facing page) is to glue rigid polystyrene foam board directly to the walls. A big advantage of this approach is that this kind of insulation serves as its own vapor retardant, thereby solving the riddle of vapor-retardant placement encountered with the stud wall. Rigid foam insulation keeps moist interior air from coming into contact with the cold foundation surface, thus eliminating a major source of basement condensation.

The approach shown here involves attaching furring strips for drywall or paneling on top of the insulation, but you may be able to find rigid foam products made specifically for basement walls that have channels along the edges for furring strips. The channels permit the furring strips to be installed flush with the face of the insulation.

1 Gluing the Boards

Cut the boards to fit as snugly as possible around pipes and other obstructions, then lay a serpentine bead of exterior-grade adhesive to each board and press it against the wall. Fill any gaps with caulk or spray foam. Always use products recommended by the manufacturer of the foam board for sealing and gluing.

2 Adding Furring Strips

With the foam boards in place, attach 1 by 3 furring strips at 24-inch intervals, using a level to keep each one vertical. Drive masonry nails through the furring strip and the insulation, then into the foundation masonry. You can then fasten drywall to the furring strips.

INSULATING CONCRETE FLOORS

An uninsulated concrete floor in a finished basement or garage lets valuable heat escape from your house. The technique described here for insulating such a floor sacrifices the finish flooring—you can roll up wall-to-wall carpet and re-lay it later—to create a plywood subfloor you can cover as you choose.

Because the materials are rigid, it's best to insulate a basement or garage floor on a clean,

relatively flat slab, although it's possible to grind minor high spots flat with an abrasive block. Do not insulate a basement floor that is often wet; tend to the moisture problem first. If the floor is sloped toward a drain, talk with a contractor before proceeding.

Keep in mind, too, that building codes often require the distance between finished floor and finished ceiling to be at least 7 feet 6 inches. An insulated subfloor will

reduce headroom in the garage or basement by at least 2 inches.

Heat also escapes through the edges of a concrete slab foundation, so insulate them as well. Dig a trench around the perimeter at least 6 inches deep. Clean the sides of the slab and attach rigid foam insulation. Then cover the insulation with pressure-treated plywood, a cement coating, or another protective layer before filling in the trench.

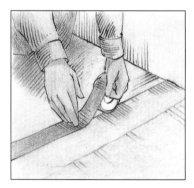

1 Preparing the Floor

Vacuum the floor thoroughly. If the insulation you have chosen requires a vapor retardant, cover the floor with 6-mil polyethylene sheeting. Overlap seams at least 6 inches and tape them. On a basement floor, run the vapor retardant up the walls several inches. To keep the polyethylene from slipping on the floor, stick it to the concrete with dabs of caulk.

2 Adding Sleepers and Foam

Arrange pressure-treated 2 by 4 sleepers end to end around the perimeter of the floor. Fasten the sleepers to the floor with a powder-actuated nailer or 2¼-inch masonry nails. Then install a gridiron of sleepers across the floor, centered every 16 inches. Cut panels of 4-feet-wide and 1½-inch-thick rigid foam insulation into three 12½-inch-wide strips. Lay the strips between the sleepers.

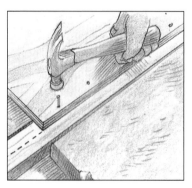

3 Attaching the Subfloor

Lay ¾-inch plywood perpendicular to the sleepers. To stagger the seams between panels, begin every other row with a half sheet of plywood. Fasten the plywood to the 2 by 4s with 2-inch ringshank nails or 2-inch galvanized screws.

INSULATING HOT WATER PIPES

Hot water cools on the way from the water heater to faucets, shower heads, and other outlets. The best way to minimize this heat loss is to insulate as much of the hot water piping as you can reach. It's also important to insulate 3 feet or so of the cold water supply pipe where it enters the water heater.

There are two kinds of insulation made for pipes—foam sleeves and foam insulation tape. You can insulate straight sections of pipe as well as bends and turns with either kind of insulation. Sometimes, however, the best strategy is to sleeve the straight sections and use tape for the turns, using duct tape to seal seams where the two materials meet.

When shopping for pipe insulation, look for foam sleeves that are slit to accept the pipe and that have an integral adhesive strip to seal the seam. Buy sleeves that fit the outside diameter of your hot water pipes, which may vary. R-values of sleeves vary with the thickness of the foam; get the thickest sleeves that you can slip around your pipes and that clear the walls or framing of your house.

Insulation tape comes with either a foil backing or plas-tic wrap that you wind around the pipes on top of the fiberglass. Like foam sleeves, the tape can be difficult to install in tight spaces.

Insulating a Straight Run with Foam Sleeves

Measure the length of pipe to be covered, then cut sleeves to fit. Open the slit in a sleeve at one end and slip it onto the pipe. Then fit the rest of the sleeve over the pipe, butting ends tightly against neighboring sleeves. Seal the joints between sleeves with duct tape.

Sleeving a Corner

For 90-degree turns, miter the ends of two sleeves at a 45-degree angle, then install them so that the miters fit tightly together. (Some foam sleeves have one mitered end, which can save you the trouble of making the cuts yourself.) Tape the joint. At a T joint, cut two 45-degree miters on one end of a third section of sleeve.

Wrapping Pipes in Tape

Clean and dry the pipe, then wrap the insulation tape carefully around it, overlapping the edges as you go. Secure the ends with duct tape, or with the tape that comes with the insulation. Cover the pipe completely, paying special attention at turns. Take care not to compress the insulation by pulling it too tight. Cover the insulation with plastic wrap, if supplied, then secure the plastic with tape.

A BLANKET FOR A WATER HEATER

Heating water is an expensive proposition, accounting for 15 to 40 percent of a household's utility bill. Wrapping your water heater with an insulation blanket can save some of this money by slowing the drop in temperature of hot water as it sits unused in the water heater. With the water staying hotter longer, the water heater remains off more of the time, saving you energy and money.

Not all water heaters need a blanket. Newer, energy-efficient models have a thick layer of insulation inside the tank that is suffi-cient without extra insulation.

Insulation blankets for water heaters less protected against heat loss are available at home centers and hardware stores. Installing one is not much different from putting on a coat, although it usually requires a little cutting and trimming for a satisfactory fit. You can minimize such adjustments with an insulation blanket that is sized according to how many gallons of water the tank holds.

Before adding the blanket, inspect all of the water-heater fittings, especially where they pass through the wall of the tank. If you find any leaks or signs of deterioration, have a plumber make the necessary repairs before proceeding. And be sure to read the instructions and warnings provided by the blanket manufacturer (see facing page).

Adding an Insulation Blanket

Remove the insulation blanket from the package and wrap it around the tank to see how it fits. On gas units, insulate only the sides of the tank; the insulation could hinder the flow of exhaust gases out the top. On electric units, however, you can insulate the top as well.

With a heavy-duty scissors or a utility knife, make cutouts in the blanket for the drain valve, thermostat, and other fittings (facing page). If you wish, you can also cut the blanket to expose safety and warning labels on the tank. Tape around the cutouts and along the seam where the blanket meets itself after encircling the water heater.

A Safe Insulation

Some manufacturers warn against adding an insulation blanket to their water heaters. Primarily, they are concerned about unsafe installations that, among other things, cover warning labels. The illustrations below show how to safely wrap both gas and electric units. If your water heater is still under warranty, however, check the printed material that came with the unit to make sure that insulating the tank doesn't void the warranty.

Check the Thermostat
Water heaters often leave the factory with the thermostat set as high as 140ºF. The installer or previous homeowner may have set it even higher. By turning the thermostat down to about 120ºF, you can significantly reduce energy bills, as well as the danger of scalds from overheated water.

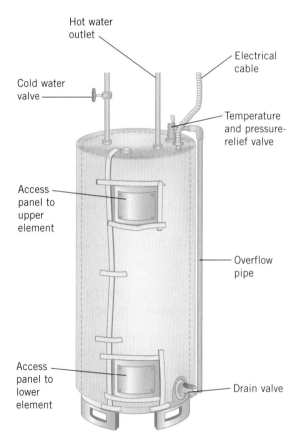

Hot water outlet

Electrical cable

Cold water valve

Temperature and pressure-relief valve

Access panel to upper element

Overflow pipe

Access panel to lower element

Drain valve

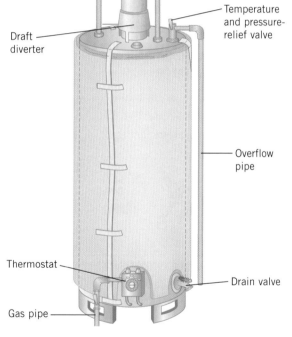

Cold water valve

Flue pipe

Temperature and pressure-relief valve

Draft diverter

Overflow pipe

Thermostat

Drain valve

Gas pipe

Electric Water Heaters

The top and the full length of the sides of an electric water heater can be covered with insulation. The access panels to the upper and lower elements should be left exposed on the sides, as should the junction box for electrical connections on top.

Gas Water Heaters

The insulation blanket must not block combustion air to the burner of a gas water heater or impede the flow of exhaust gases through the flue. For these reasons, the bottom of the blanket should extend no more than a couple of inches below the drain valve. And the top of the tank should be left free of insulation.

IMPROVEMENTS THAT LOWER HOT WATER COSTS

Paying more than you need for hot water is the same as pouring energy dollars down the drain. Here and on the following pages, you'll find hands-on instructions that show you how to fix leaky faucets, install water-conserving devices, and investigate more economical ways of heating water—plus two energy-efficient suggestions for getting hot water where you need it. Over time, you can expect energy savings to repay your investment in these measures, sometimes generously.

ADDING A MONEY-SAVING FAUCET AERATOR

A faucet aerator works by mixing air into the water stream. The result is a high-pressure flow that uses less water than a solid stream. An added benefit is that  an aerated stream does not splash.

In normal household use, aerators installed on all your kitchen and bathroom faucets can save the BTUs needed to heat several hundred gallons of hot water a year. For maximum effect, look for a kitchen aerator rated for a flow of 2.5 gallons per minute (GPM) or less, and for a bathroom aerator rated as low as 1 GPM.

Replacement aerators are generally made to fit faucets with spouts that are threaded either on the inside or the outside. Some swivel so that you can direct the stream where you wish; others have a built-in control that allows you to interrupt the flow without also affecting water temperature.

An aerator comes with a rubber or plastic washer. To install the aerator on a spout with inside threads, place the washer on the aerator; discard the washer when fitting the aerator to a spout with outside threads. Screw the aerator on hand tight. (If the faucet and aerator threads don't match, purchase an adapter from your local home center or plumbing supply dealer.)

REPLACING A WASTEFUL SHOWER HEAD

Installing a low-flow shower head rated at no more than 2.5 GPM can be one of the most effective ways to save money spent to heat water. Start by taping the jaws of a pipe wrench to avoid marring shiny finishes. Use the wrench to keep the shower arm from turning while you unscrew the old shower head using an adjustable wrench or a second taped pipe wrench.

The new shower head screws directly onto the shower arm

unless it has a ball joint at the end. In that case, you'll need a standard half-inch threaded shower head adapter. To install the adapter, wrap one end with pipe-thread tape and screw it tightly into the ball joint.

Apply pipe-thread tape to the shower arm or the other end of the adapter, then screw on the new shower head hand tight using any washers supplied by the manufacturer. If water leaks from the joint, tighten the new shower head with the tools you used to loosen the old one.

WATER HEATER MAINTENANCE

Keeping your water heater free of sediment makes it work more efficiently and is especially important if you live in an area with hard—mineral-laden—water. Keeping the water temperature at 120°F or lower slows sediment accumulation, yet the water is hot enough for most household purposes. Only a dishwasher requires hotter water, but many of these appliances can raise the water temperature to 140°F.

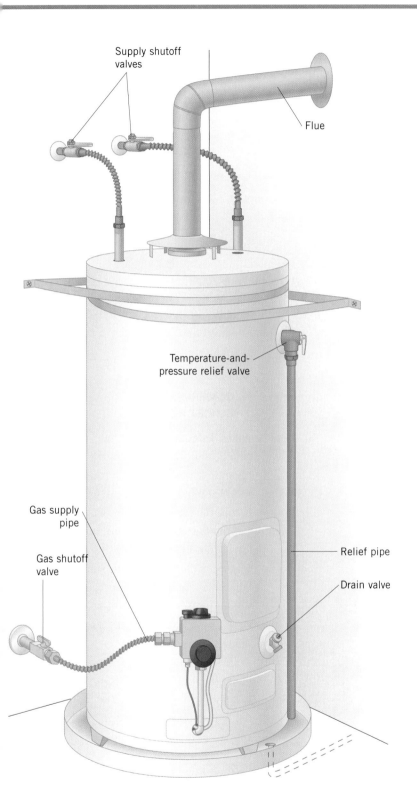

Supply shutoff valves

Flue

Temperature-and-pressure relief valve

Gas supply pipe

Gas shutoff valve

Relief pipe

Drain valve

To drain sediment, first turn off the water supply to the heater at the cold water intake pipe or at the house's main shut-off valve. If yours is a gas-fired heater, turn the temperature control knob to OFF and close the shut-off valve to the gas supply line. With an electric heater, turn off power at the main service panel.

Next, attach a length of garden hose to the drain valve and lead the other end to a floor drain or outdoors below the level of the heater. Alternatively, place a bucket or tub under the drain.

Open the drain valve and a nearby hot water faucet to let air into the system. When the water flowing from the tank looks clear, close the valve. If the water remains cloudy until the tank is empty, turn on the cold water supply valve for a few minutes to flush remaining sediment.

Close the drain valve and the nearby hot water faucet. If you have not already opened the cold water supply valve, do so now to refill the tank. When you can no longer hear water flowing into the tank, restore electric power or open the gas line and relight the pilot light if there is one. Set the thermostat to 120°F or lower.

FIXING LEAKY FAUCETS

Faucets can leak in two ways—a steady drip from the spout or a relentless seeping from the stem that leaves a telltale puddle beneath the faucet handle. In either case, it's time for a repair.

If possible, determine the make and model of faucet before starting work. Your home center or plumbing supply dealer stocks repair kits for most faucets. A kit contains replacement parts, instructions, and—if necessary—special tools for disassembling the faucet. If you don't know what kind of faucet you have, take the defective parts to the dealer for matching replacements.

Shutting Off the Water

Before beginning any plumbing repair, close the fixture's shutoff valves—you can usually find them where the supply lines to the faucet come out of the wall—and open the faucet to drain it. If there are no shutoff valves, turn ff the water at the house's main valve, then open the lowest faucet in the house to drain the supply lines. When you have finished a repair, turn on the water and check your work for leaks.

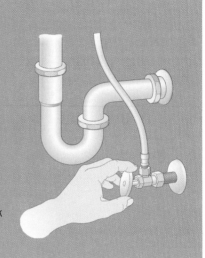

COMPRESSION FAUCET REPAIR

A sink, bathtub, or shower has compression faucets if there are separate hot and cold water handles that require increasing effort to turn the water all the way off.

Whatever its size or shape, this kind of faucet has a rubber seat washer on the end of a brass stem. When you turn the faucet off, the washer presses against a brass valve seat in the faucet body, stopping the flow.

To keep water from leaking under the handle when the faucet is running, the stem has a stem nut that compresses a washer, O-ring, or graphite-impregnated twine that serves as a seal. Water can leak past the seat washer or around the packing. Either kind of leak is easy to repair.

Trim cap

Handle

Stem nut

Stem

Packing

Threads

Seat washer

Screw

Valve seat

Faucet body

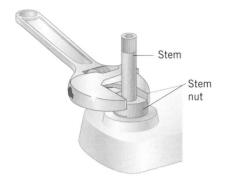

Take Out the Stem

Remove the handle either by prying gently around the base or by removing a screw under the trim cap. Using a properly fitting wrench, take off the stem nut, then unscrew the stem in the direction that would turn the faucet on. If necessary, use the faucet handle as a wrench.

Renew the Packing

If water leaks around the handle—or to forestall a leak there—replace the packing washer, O-ring, or twine. Reassemble the faucet, snugging down the stem nut until the stem begins to bind, then loosen the nut slightly.

Replace the Seat Washer

If water drips from the spout, take out the screw in the base of the stem, and pry off the seat washer. Inspect the lip around the stem base and the threads for the screw that holds the seat washer. If both are sound, replace the seat washer with an exact duplicate. If not, substitute a snap-in swivel-head washer of the correct diameter.

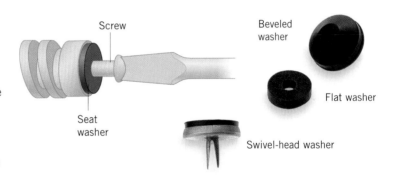

Check the Valve Seat

Use a valve-seat wrench to unscrew the faucet valve seat, then inspect it. If it is worn or chipped, replace it with a duplicate. In older faucets, the seat may not be removable, but you can restore the sealing surface with a valve-seat dresser. Insert the tool and turn it clockwise until the seat is bright and smooth. Remove any metal shavings with a damp cloth.

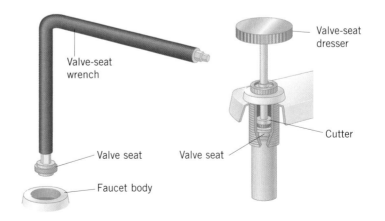

■ DISC FAUCET REPAIR

Washerless faucets, which control the flow and the mix of hot and cold water with a single handle, have replaceable seals inside.

The first step in repairing any washerless faucet is to remove the handle. If it has an external setscrew, use a properly fitting screwdriver or hex wrench to loosen it, then lift the handle off. If the handle has a trim cap, pry it off and remove the screw it hides.

Underneath the handle a cap is threaded to the faucet body. Removing the cap with tape-wrapped pliers provides access to the internal assembly.

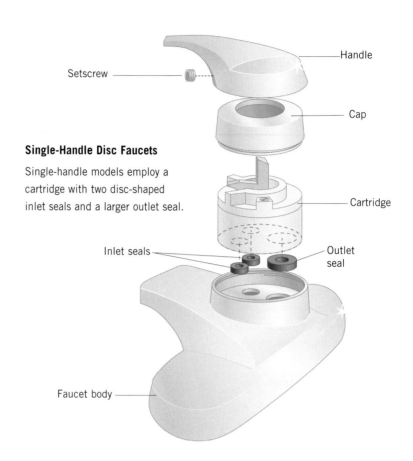

Single-Handle Disc Faucets

Single-handle models employ a cartridge with two disc-shaped inlet seals and a larger outlet seal.

Replacing the Seals

Loosen the screws that fasten the cartridge to the faucet body and lift out the cartridge. Replace the worn seals and reassemble, aligning the seals with corresponding holes and any lugs in the cartridge with slots in the faucet body.

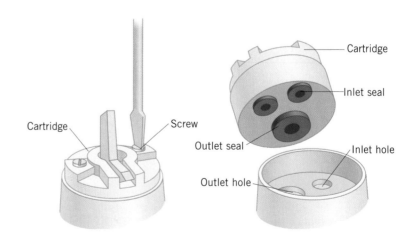

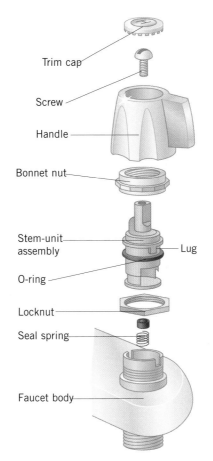

Trim cap

Screw

Handle

Bonnet nut

Double-Handle Disc Faucets

Two-handle models operate the same as single-handle models except for having a stem-unit assembly with a spring-loaded seal.

Stem-unit assembly

Lug

O-ring

Locknut

Seal spring

Faucet body

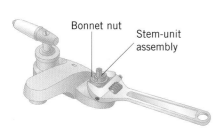

Bonnet nut

Stem-unit assembly

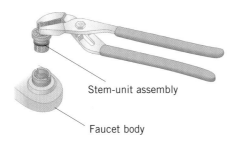

Stem-unit assembly

Faucet body

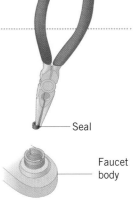

Seal

Faucet body

1 **Disassemble the Faucet**

Remove the handle and bonnet nut.

2 **Replace the O-Ring**

Pull out the stem-unit assembly with pliers and remove the O-ring. Lubricate a new O-ring with silicone grease and slip it into its groove in the assembly. Use your fingers; a tool can damage the O-ring.

3 **Replace the Seal and Spring**

Gently lift out the old seal and spring with pliers and replace them. Reinstall the stem-unit assembly, aligning any lugs in the stem with slots in the faucet body.

■ BALL FAUCETS

In a ball faucet, the seals are located in the faucet body and held in place by a movable brass or plastic ball to which the handle is attached.

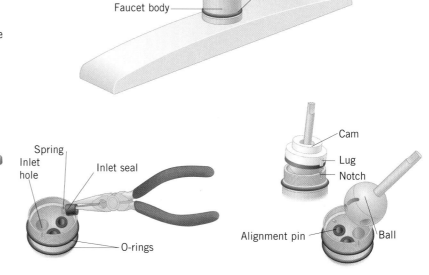

Handle — Setscrew
Adjusting ring
Cap
Spout sleeve
Cam
Cam washer
Ball
Seal   Spring   Spout O-rings
Faucet body

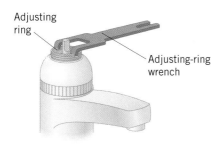

Adjusting ring
Adjusting-ring wrench

1 Tightening the Ring

If the faucet leaks around the handle, tighten the adjusting ring with the two-pronged wrench from the repair kit.

Tape   Cap

Spout sleeve

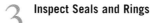

Spring
Inlet hole
Inlet seal
O-rings

Cam
Lug
Notch
Alignment pin   Ball

2 Disassemble the Faucet

To fix a spout drip, unscrew the cap with tape-wrapped pliers, pull the spout sleeve off the faucet body, and lift out the cam and ball.

3 Inspect Seals and Rings

Using long-nosed pliers, remove the old seals and springs, wipe the inlet and outlet holes clean, and insert new parts from the repair kit. If the O-rings on the faucet body appear worn, replace them with new ones lubricated with silicone grease.

4 Replace the Ball and Cam

Install the new ball that comes with the repair kit, aligning the slot in the ball with the pin in the faucet body. Reassemble with a new cam and cam washer, aligning the lug on the cam with the corresponding notch in the faucet body. Reassemble, tightening the adjusting ring just short of causing the ball to bind.

■ CARTRIDGE FAUCETS

These faucets, which are used in both sinks and showers, have a stem-and-cartridge assembly sealed with O-rings.

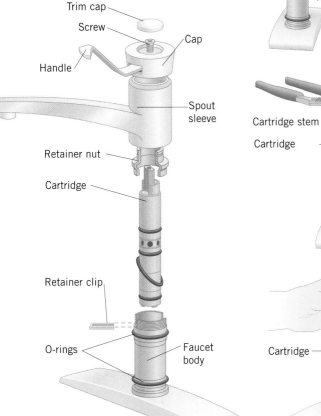

Trim cap
Screw
Handle
Cap
Spout sleeve
Retainer nut
Cartridge
Retainer clip
O-rings
Faucet body

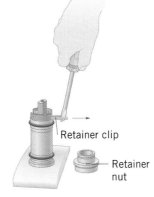

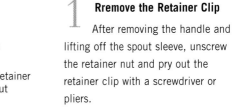

Retainer clip
Retainer nut

1 Rremove the Retainer Clip

After removing the handle and lifting off the spout sleeve, unscrew the retainer nut and pry out the retainer clip with a screwdriver or pliers.

Cartridge stem
Cartridge

2 Replace the O-Rings

Using pliers to grip the stem, pull the cartridge straight up; you may need to pull hard. Replace worn O-rings with new rings lubricated with silicone grease.

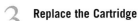

Flat side
Cartridge

3 Replace the Cartridge

Reinstall the cartridge. Push it firmly into the faucet body, keeping the flat side of the stem facing forward. Replace the retainer clip and nut, then the spout sleeve and handle.

■ SHOWER FAUCETS

When repairing a cartridge-type shower control, you may have to chip away the surrounding wall under the escutcheon to insert a shower socket and unscrew the retainer nut. Replace the O-rings or the entire cartridge as described above.

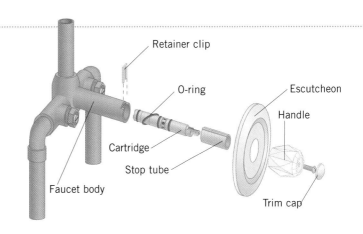

Retainer clip
O-ring
Escutcheon
Handle
Cartridge
Stop tube
Trim cap
Faucet body

ON-DEMAND WATER HEATERS

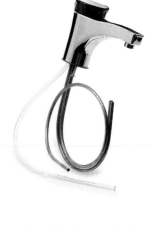

If your water heater is a long way from the kitchen sink, an on-demand hot water dispenser can be a real energy saver. The dispenser has a tank that holds about ½ gallon of water. Inside, an electric heating element keeps the water at a temperature between 160°F and 190°F. The unit recovers quickly after hot water is drawn off and generally costs much less to operate than heating water that cools unused in hot-water supply pipes.

Installation is simple. Begin by inserting the dispenser's faucet through a standard 1¼-inch hole precut in most sinks—or bore a hole through the countertop where the faucet spout will over-hang the sink. Secure the faucet by tightening the retaining nut beneath the countertop.

Next, attach the tank to the inside of the cabinet or to the wall beneath the faucet near a grounded receptacle. If no receptacle is available, install one or have an electrician do the work. In either case, protect the receptacle with a ground fault circuit interrupter (GFCI) to prevent electric shock.

Connect one of the faucet's two shorter lengths of ¼-inch copper tubing to the cold water inlet on the tank and the other to the hot water outlet. Some units have a plastic vent line; slip it over the tank's vent fitting.

Using the self-tapping supply valve that comes with the unit, connect the longer piece of copper tubing to the cold water supply pipe. For a more substantial installation, a T-fitting and shutoff valve can be soldered to the supply line.

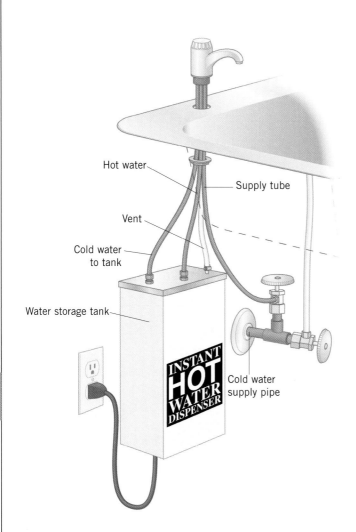

Hot water

Supply tube

Vent

Cold water to tank

Water storage tank

INSTANT HOT WATER DISPENSER

Cold water supply pipe

Hot Water from the Sun

Heating water is one of the most practical ways to harness the sun's energy. A well-designed solar hot water system can supply between 60 and 90 percent of a household's hot water needs.

The heart of a solar hot water system is the solar collector panel—an insulated, weatherproof aluminum box about 4 feet wide and 6 to 10 feet

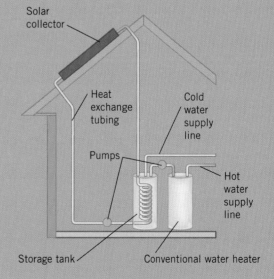

Clear plastic cover

Out

Heat-exchange tubing

Heat absorbing panel

In

long (above). The box has a black, heat-absorbing panel on the bottom and a top made of clear plastic. Inside is an array of heat-exchange tubing to absorb heat from the sun. Also painted black, the tubing is often fitted with fins like an automobile radiator to capture as much solar energy as possible. One or more solar collector panels are normally installed on a roof or in another unshaded, elevated location, facing southward to bask in as much direct sunlight as possible throughout the year.

In one kind of solar heating system—called a direct system because the water that flows through the collectors eventually flows from the tap—water from a cold water supply pipe flows into the collector. As it does,

the sun heats it to a temperature as high as 140°F. From the collector, the hot water is piped to an insulated storage tank, often located inside the house. Because the collectors are filled with water in a direct system, such an arrangement is only practical where there is no threat of freezing winter temperatures.

Climates with harsher winters require an indirect, or closed-loop, system (below, right). It works on a similar principle, but instead of water it pumps a low-freezing-point fluid through the collector's heat-exchange tubing, which then coils inside or around an insulated storage tank. As the hot fluid circulates through the coil, it transfers its heat to the water in the storage tank.

In direct and indirect systems alike, a pipe from the storage tank leads to the cold water inlet of the existing water heater. In a passive delivery system, gravity carries water from the storage tank to the water heater lower in the house. An active delivery system has a pump to circulate the heated water from the storage tank to the water heater. Electricity for any pumps in the system

can come from a photovoltaic panel installed beside the solar collectors.

Once installed, the solar water heater works in concert with the existing one. Whenever a hot water faucet is opened somewhere in the house, hot water that flows from the water heater is replaced by preheated water from the storage tank. If the solar collectors cannot satisfy the demand for hot water—at night or on cloudy days, for example—the water heater fires up when the temperature of the water inside falls below the thermostat setting.

Before investing in any solar hot water system, have a heating consultant evaluate the potential savings and determine the system type and capacity best suited to your family's needs. A simple direct system can be constructed and hooked into your water supply for well under $1,000. An indirect system will cost from $2,000 to $5,000 or more.

Solar collector

Heat exchange tubing

Cold water supply line

Pumps

Hot water supply line

Storage tank

Conventional water heater

RESOURCES

▪ GOVERNMENT SOURCES

U. S. Department of Energy
EREC
P.O. Box 3048
Merrifield, VA 22116
800/363-3732
703/893-0400
www.energy.gov

Energy Savers
Tips on saving energy and money
at home. Produced by the United
States Department of Energy's
Office of Building Technology and
state and community programs.
www.eren.doe.gov/consumerinfo

Energy Star
888/782-7937
www.energystar.gov

California
www.ca.gov.state/portal/
myca_homepage

California Energy Commission
www.energy.ca.gov

Consumer Energy Information
www.eren.doe.gov/consumerinfo/
forhome.html

TVA and Local Power Companies
Energy Right Program
www.energyright.com

▪ ORGANIZATIONS

Alliance to Save Energy
1200 18th Street, NW
Suite 900
Washington, DC 20036
202/857-0666
202/331-9588
www.ase.org

**The American Council for an
Energy Efficient Economy**
1001 Connecticut Avenue, NW
Suite 801
Washington, DC 20036
www.aceee.org

**Appliance.Com Consumer
Connection**
www.appliance.com

ENERGYguide
6 Laurel Avenue
Suite 100
Wellesley Hills, MA 02481
781/283-9160
781/283-9150
www.energyguide.com/energy

▪ UTILITY COMPANIES

ComEd
www.ceco.com

Florida Power and Light
www.fpl.com/

Pacific Gas & Electric Company
www.pge.com

Pepco
Home Power Net
www.pepco.com

San Diego Gas & Electric
www.sdge.com

Southern California Edison
www.sce.com

▪ COMMERCE

Buylighting.com
72 North 22nd Avenue
Minneapolis, MN 55411
888/990-9933
www.buylighting.com

The Home Depot
2455 Paces Ferry Road
Atlanta, GA 30339
800/430-3376
www.homedepot.com

homestore.com: Appliances
www.homestore.com/HomeTech

Topbulb.com
800/TOP-BULB
www.800topbulb.com

▪ MANUFACTURERS

**AGA Cookers
North America**
201 Main Street
Ames, Iowa 50010
800/633-9200
515/233-2604
www.aga-cookers.com

Amana Refrigeration, Inc.
Heating and Air-Conditioning Div.
1801 Wilson Parkway
Fayetteville, TN 37334
800/843-0304
319/622-2977
www.amana.com

Asko, Inc.
1161 Executive Drive West
Richardson, TX 75081
972/644-8024
www.askousa.com

Bosch Home Appliances
5551 McFadden Avenue
Huntington Beach, CA 92649
800/944-2904
www.boschappliances.com

Carrier Corporation
c/o ACLS
108 Metropolitan Park Drive
Liverpool, NY 13088-5112
800/962-9212
www.global.carrier.com

Casablanca Fan Company
450 N. Baldwin Park Blvd.
City of Industry, CA 91746
818/369-6441
818/633-1293
www.casablancafanco.com

Dacor
950 S. Raymond Avenue
Pasadena, CA 91105
800/793-0093
818/799-1000
www.dacorappl.com

Equator Corporation
Equator Plaza
10067 Timber Oak Drive
Houston, Texas 77080-7045
713/464-3422
800/935-1955
www.equatorappliances.com

Fisher & Paykel Appliances, Inc.
22982 Alcalde Drive
Suite 201
Laguna Hills, CA 92653
800/863-5394
www.fisherpaykel.com

Frigidaire Company
Electrolux Home Products
P.O. Box 212378
Martinez, GA 30917
800/444-4944
706/860-4110
www.frigidaire.com

GE Appliances
Appliance Park
Louisville, KY 40225
800/626-2000
www.geappliances.com

GE Lighting
www.gelighting.com

Honeywell,Inc.
Honeywell Plaza
Minneapolis, MN 55408
www.honeywell.com/yourhome

Hunter Fan Company
2500 Frisco Avenue
Memphis, TN 38114
901/743-1360
www.hunterfan.com

Jenn-Air
One Dependability Square
Newton, IA 50208
800/688-9900
www.jennair.com

KitchenAid
800/422-1230
www.KitchenAid.com

Lennox Industries, Inc.
P.O. Box 799900
Dallas, TX 75379-9900
214/497-5000
www.davelennox.com

Maytag Appliances
One Dependability Square
Newton, IA 50208
800/688-9900
www.maytag.com

Miele, Inc.
9 Independence Way
Princeton, NJ 08540
800/463-0260
609/419-9898
www.miele.com

Owens Corning
www.owenscorning.com

Rheem Mfg. Company
405 Lexington Avenue
22nd Floor
New York, NY 10174-0307
212/916-8100
www.rheem.com

Royal Philips Electronics
800/326-6586
www.philips.com
www.lighting.philips.com

The Trane Company
6200 Troup Highway
Tyler, TX 75711
903/581-9070
www.trane.com

Sub-Zero Freezer Company, Inc.
P.O. Box 44130
4717 Hammersley Road
Madison, WI 53744-4130
608/271-2233 or 800/222-7820
www.subzero.com

Thermador
5551 McFadden Avenue
Huntington Beach, CA 92649
800/656-9226
www.thermador.com

Viking Range Corporation
111 Front Street
Greenwood, MS 38930
888/845-4641
601/455-1200
www.vikingrange.com

Weber-Stephen Products Company
200 East Daniels Road
Palatine, IL 60067-6266
708/934-5700
www.weber.com

Whirlpool Corporation
1714 Heil-Quaker Boulevard
LaVergne, TN 37086-1985
800/253-1301
www.whirlpoolcorp.com

Wolf Range Company
19600 S. Alameda
Compton, CA 90221-6291
800/366-WOLF
www.wolfrange.com

York International
Central Environmental Systems
Division
P.O. Box 1592-232F
York, PA 17405
717/771-6197
www.york.com

Air shutter: On a gas range, the valve that controls the amount of air that reaches a burner.

Baseboard heater: An electric heat source, either plug-in or permanently installed, located along the bottom of a wall.

Batts and blankets: Fiberglass insulation in 4-foot-long sections (batts) or long rolls (blankets).

Caulk: A compound used to seal seams and joints against water or air infiltration. Caulk comes in tubes, and is applied using a caulking gun. Caulk is often composed of latex, silicone, or a combination of the two.

Cellulose: Fluffy wood-based material often used for insulation.

CFL (compact fluorescent lamp): A fluorescent light source that can be screwed into a standard incandescent lamp or light fixture.

CFM (cubic feet per minute): A rating that tells the volume of air a fan can move.

Circuit breaker: A safety switch in a service panel that breaks the flow of electricity by tripping off when a circuit is overloaded.

Condensation: The formation of water that occurs when warm, moist air meets a cooler surface.

Convector: A type of radiator, common in newer homes, made of copper pipe and radiant fins.

Dehumidifier: An appliance that condenses moisture out of the air and collects it in a tray for disposal.

Double- and triple-glazed windows: Windows made with two or three panes separated from each other by a thin space filled with inert gas to provide insulation.

Electrical box: A plastic or metal container that houses electrical connections.

Electroluminescent: Light that results from a discharge of electricity through a gas.

Fiberglass: Small threads of spun glass used to make insulating batts or blankets.

Fluorescent light: A fixture that produces ultraviolet light by bombarding mercury vapor in a glass tube with a small amount of electricity. The ultraviolet rays strike a coating on the interior surface of the tube, producing visible light. Fluorescent tubes use far less energy than incandescent bulbs.

Fuse: A safety device in a service panel that interrupts the flow of electricity when a circuit is overloaded.

Gasket: A seal that prevents a liquid or a gas from passing through a joint between adjoining surfaces, for example, the flexible magnetic seal on a refrigerator or the heat-resistant seal on an oven door.

GFCI (ground-fault circuit interrupter): An electrical safety device found in some receptacles and circuit breakers that shuts off power when it senses electricity flowing in the wrong direction.

Humidifier: An appliance that disperses moisture into the air.

IC (insulation-contact) fixture: A light fixture whose housing remains cool enough that it can be installed directly against ceiling insulation. A non-IC requires 3 inches of open space between it and any insulation.

Incandescent bulb: A device that produces light by heating a filament white-hot.

Insulation: Material used to isolate cold or hot outside air from a home's interior. See Cellulose; Fiberglass; Batts and Blankets.

Insulation (electrical): Material that does not carry electrical current, such as the color-coded thermoplastic sleeve on wires.

Joist: A horizontal framing member, usually 2 by 6 or larger, used to support ceilings and floors. Joists are usually placed at 16-inch intervals.

Kilowatt: A unit of electrical power equal to 1,000 watts. Abbreviated kW.

Knockout: In an electrical box or fixture, a pre-stamped circular flap that can be left in place or removed for a cable to enter.

Loose-fill insulation: Fibrous material, usually made of cellulose, rock wool, or fiberglass, that can be blown into the spaces between joists and wall studs.

Low-E (low-emissivity) glass: Glass panes treated with an invisible coating that blocks much of the sun's ultraviolet radiation. Usually, the coating is in the sealed airspace of a double-paned window.

Lumen: A unit of brightness roughly equal to the light produced by a single candle.

O-ring: A narrow rubber ring used as a gasket in some faucets to prevent leaking.

Photoelectric sensor: A switch that can turn lights on at night and off during the day according to the absence or presence of light.

Polyethylene: A type of plastic sheeting that is used to keep moist air out of insulation so that moisture doesn't condense and ruin it.

Propane (LPG): A dense flammable gas stored in tanks and used mostly in rural areas for the same purposes as natural gas. Special LPG fittings are often required.

R-value: A measure of the capacity of insulating material to resist heat flow. The higher the R-value rating, the better the material insulates.

Radiant heat: A system that heats a house by means of heating elements—usually pipes filled with heated water—running through floors. Heat radiates up through the entire floor.

Radiator: The component of a heating system that transfers heat from hot water or steam piped from a boiler to the air in a room. See also Convector.

Refrigerator condenser coils: Thin, serpentine pipes located at the bottom or rear of a refrigerator that dissipate heat removed from the refrigerator interior.

Refrigerator cooling coils: Also called evaporator coils. Coiled thin pipes located inside a freezer or in the upper portion of a refrigerator. Liquid refrigerant is pumped to the coils, where it boils and expands into a gas and removes heat from the refrigerator.

Register: In a forced-air heating-and-cooling system, an opening in a floor or wall that is covered by a grille or shutters and connected to ductwork leading to the furnace and air conditioner. A supply register admits heated or cooled air into a room; a return register routes air back to the furnace for reheating or to the air conditioner for recooling.

Rigid foam insulation: Insulating sheets, ranging from $\frac{1}{2}$ to 2 inches thick, made of polyurethane or polystyrene.

Service panel: Also called a service entrance panel or main fuse or breaker box. The main power cabinet through which electricity enters a home from the electric company's power lines and is distributed to the various circuits in the house. The service panel contains a main disconnect breaker or fuse, a circuit breaker or fuse for each circuit, and a grounding connection for the entire system.

Shim: A thin piece of wood or other material, often tapered, used to fill in a space or slightly raise an object. Wood shims are often made of cedar, tapered from $\frac{1}{8}$ to $\frac{3}{8}$ inches thick.

Skylight: A window in the roof to provide natural light to a room. Skylights are often translucent rather than clear; some can be opened to provide ventilation.

Sleepers: Wood strips, typically flat-laid 1 by 3s, that rest on a subfloor (either wood or concrete) and support tongue-and-groove or plywood flooring.

Stud: A vertical framing member, usually 2 by 4 but sometimes 2 by 6, used to construct a wall. Studs are usually placed at 16-inch intervals. Drywall or lath and plaster are attached to studs.

UL-approved: An electrical device, fixture, tool, or appliance certified as safe by the Underwriter's Laboratory, an independent testing agency.

U-value: A measure of the insulating properties of glass. The lower the U-value, the less heat is transmitted through the glass. Also called U-factor.

Vapor barrier: A continuous sheet of polyethylene, building paper, or roofing felt, typically installed in conjunction with insulation, to keep water vapor in moist air from entering the house and its insulation.

Vents: Openings in a roof or attic walls that allow the attic to "breathe," thereby preventing heat buildup in summer and condensation in winter. Vents may be placed along the ridge (the top of the roof), at gables (vertical walls in an attic), or in soffits (under the eaves). Crawl spaces and basements may need vents as well.

Volt: A unit of electrical pressure. Most household lights and appliances operate on 120 volts; electric ovens, clothes dryers, and some other appliances use 240 volts. Abbreviated V.

Washer: A flat, thin ring of metal or rubber used to ensure a tight fit and prevent friction in plumbing joints and assemblies.

Watt: A unit of measurement for electrical power. Abbreviated W.

Weatherstripping: Long, thin material installed to seal out cold or hot air from a window or door. Weatherstripping may be made of foam, rubber, felt, metal, or wood.

Whole-house fan: A large fan located in the highest ceiling of a house. It cools the entire house by drawing outdoor air through open windows and doors and pushing it into the attic, where it exits through vents.

Window sash: A frame made of wood, metal, or plastic that contains a pane or panes of glass. In a double-hung window, at least one sash can be raised and lowered to open and close the window.

Wire nut: A plastic or plastic-and-metal connector used to splice two or more wires.